Alex Kerr is an
Japanologist. *Lost Japan* is his most famous work. He was the
first foreigner to be awarded the Shincho Gakugei Literature
Prize for the best work of non-fiction published in Japan.

Kathy Arlyn Sokol is a non-fiction author, interviewer and
Emmy award-winning narrator who has spent over thirty years
living in Kyoto. Her book *Rasta Time*, on Bob Marley's life and
legacy, will soon be released in English.

Another Kyoto

ALEX KERR
With Kathy Arlyn Sokol

PENGUIN BOOKS

PENGUIN BOOKS

UK | USA | Canada | Ireland | Australia
India | New Zealand | South Africa

Penguin Books is part of the Penguin Random House group of companies
whose addresses can be found at global.penguinrandomhouse.com.

First published in Japan by Sekaibunka Publishing Inc. 2016
First published in Great Britain by Penguin Books 2018
003

Copyright © Alex Kerr and Kathy Arlyn Sokol, 2016

Illustrations by Tetsuji Fujihara

The moral rights of the authors have been asserted

Printed and bound in Great Britain by Clays Ltd, Elcograf S.p.A.

A CIP catalogue record for this book is available from the British Library

ISBN: 978–0–141–98833–7

www.greenpenguin.co.uk

Table of Contents

Foreword

W hen I studied Chinese classics at Oxford, at the end of each term there was a terrifying event, called "Handshaking." Dressed in a medieval black frock, each student in turn would be ushered into a room lined with oil paintings, in which he found his professor along with the Master of the College, and some other dons seated at the end of a long oak table. You sat at one end of the table, the dons sat at the other, and they talked about you. Not always flatteringly.

Fresh from 1960s liberated America, I was badly equipped to handle the British dry approach to study. In

Japan I'd been imbued with Zen and old thatched farm-houses, which fit poorly with the academic fine points I was supposed to be learning. My tutors viewed me as a Japan-influenced hippy. The low point came when I was asked to write an essay on China's ancient book of divination, the *I Ching*. I discussed its historical background, the philology of the unusual characters found in its text, what later commentators had said about it—all the stuff that had been assigned in my tutorial. At the end of the essay, I wrote, "But this is just background. The main thing about the *I Ching* is that it *works*."

That was the last straw. When I walked into Hand-shaking at the end of that term, I saw grim faces at the end of the table. One of my tutors had written a letter to the dons, which was read aloud. It went on for some time. The concluding words were: "Mr. Kerr is your typical American. He lacks academic rigor. He researches only the ephemera that draw his interest; he's quick to latch on to superstitions, myths, and oddities. He waves these peculiar interpretations around as if they were sparklers. His tales are not scholarship, and they are not to be given credit, all his protestations notwithstanding."

I say this in the name of proper disclosure, because this book follows more or less in the vein of that ill-fated *I Ching* essay. The inspiration to write it came from fellow writer and longtime Kyoto resident Kathy Arlyn Sokol, with whom I've often gone on temple-viewing outings.

One day Kathy commented, "I wish we had a record of the things you say as we walk through these temples. I think our conversations should be shared with others." So we decided to create a book that wouldn't be written, but rather spoken. We sat down with a recorder, and over several years, I would talk and Kathy recorded and transcribed. She sent edited transcripts to me and I used these as the base for an expanded text, which Kathy edited again. Back and forth it went, until finally we completed these nine essays. While they've been rewritten and revised, we've tried to keep the tone closer to speech than to writing.

I've lived in Kyoto for decades, but what brought me to Kyoto was a coincidence. It was not that I had set my heart on being here. When I was quite young my family moved to Yokohama in 1964. I went to school there and later attended university in Tokyo—very far from Kyoto and Kansai. While in university, I discovered Iya Valley in Shikoku and later bought an old thatched farmhouse in the Iya mountains, a house that became my passion. I used to commute between Tokyo and Iya, with Kyoto being just a place I passed through on the way.

I don't think I would ever have come to live in Kyoto except that I met art collector David Kidd, who became my mentor. David, who had lived in a Ming palace in Beijing before coming to Japan in the early 1950s, was a connoisseur and a great wit. He's much quoted in this book. In 1976, David founded a program of traditional arts at Oomoto Foundation, located in Kameoka, a town at the western edge of Kyoto, and he asked me to come and help out with the Oomoto school. Without realizing what I was getting into, I obeyed David, came to Oomoto, and had a life-changing discovery of Tea ceremony, Noh drama, martial arts, and so on. A year later, after graduating university, I took a job at Oomoto's International Department. In 1977 I moved into an old house in Kameoka—and I've been here ever since.

Living just outside of Kyoto, I found myself regularly going into the city. In those days it was a different place from Kyoto today. There were many beautiful old houses still standing. The temples hadn't been polished to the state in which we see them now. They were dingier, darker, but there were fewer rules about what rooms you could enter and whether you could take a photo or not. You could get up close to an old ink painting hung in a murky *tokonoma* alcove that turned out to be a masterpiece, or push open a door along a corridor and find a secret garden beyond it.

Kyoto is very much on the world tourism route, so I always had a lot of visitors. Anyone who lives here finds that they are constantly taking guests to visit temples. Since I had to do these tours so often, I came up with a "Three-to-One" policy. Each time visiting friends and I went out, we would go to the three famous places they wanted to see, and then to one place that I wanted to see. It might be a minor temple I'd read about somewhere, or a little-visited back garden within the grounds of a famous place. Discoveries could be found just a few steps off the well-beaten tourist path.

"Three-to-One" was a way to relieve the monotony of always traipsing to see the same clichéd sites. Yet repeatedly brought back to these sites for the sake of my visitors, I learned that there's an "off-the-beaten path" way to look at even the most famous landmarks. Standing yet again at tourist-clogged Kiyomizu or Kinkakuji, in my boredom I'd look away from where I'd always looked before, and I would notice something; like the little "roofs" sheltering the ends of all the wooden crossbeams sticking out from the framework beneath Kiyomizu's verandah. That made me think about roofs. And suddenly the familiar old place looked new.

Confucius said, "When I reached sixty, my ears were in order" (六十而耳順). I always thought that an odd remark. But as the years went by, I realized that you needed to look and look again before these places would unlock their secrets. One could call it "getting one's eyes in order." For one temple, the experience might be gradual, like a photographic image emerging in a chemical bath in the darkroom. For another, a new way of looking would come in one "Ah hah!" moment.

I once saw hanging in a tearoom a calligraphy with words by Zen master Dogen that said, "In all the world, there's nothing really hidden" (遍界無曾蔵). Everything we need to know is right there in front of us if we would just look at it. Likewise, most of the insights that Kathy and I arrived at turned out to be nothing very secret. It was just a matter of revisiting the obvious.

For example, before you talk about Kyoto, you need to start with Japan. That would seem obvious enough. Well, what *was* Japan? It was the end of the line of the Silk Road. For millennia, people and objects, knowledge and cultural traditions, religion and philosophy flowed here from Persia, India, Tibet, Korea, China, Java, Siam, and the South Seas.

Japan, a group of islands removed from the turmoil of the continent, took these things and slowly polished them. As centuries went by, Buddhism vanished from India, Chinese dynasties came and went, but their cultural treasures, like time capsules packed off and sent to another planet, survived destruction in their countries of origin—in Japan. This country ended up as a giant storehouse of ancient Asian wisdom. Within Japan, for a thousand years Kyoto was the capital, and so, compressed into this small space, the best and most precious were further refined.

The Meiji Restoration came along in 1868, and Japan modernized. It began to lose its link to that tradition, but one city had the critical mass of weavers, dyers, Tea ceremony schools, Noh drama, Zen temples, and Shinto shrines, and cocooned within these protective shells, the knowledge of old things survived in Kyoto. The treasure house at the end of the Silk Road that had been Japan shrank down to the treasure chest of Kyoto, making this city urgently important for anybody interested in Asian culture. It's all here.

In the process of doing this book, it became clear that the themes of Kyoto are truly endless. Kathy and I could easily do another nine essays. In fact we *did* do another set, but reluctantly put them aside so that this book could be of manageable length. Maybe one day, we'll polish up the remaining essays for a new edition.

This book is neither a coherent history nor a summing up of everything important about Kyoto, nor even about one particular temple. I don't go into much detail about the facts of things. Actually, that's not right. The book is bursting with facts, but only the ones that were helpful in taking me and Kathy into the byways we wanted to explore. For a thoroughgoing introduction to Kyoto, I recommend John Dougill's *Kyoto: A Cultural History*, with its detailed historical outline, and Gouverneur Mosher's enchanting *Kyoto: A Contemplative Guide*, which tells the tales of twelve famous places.

Another thing I remember from my Oxford days is a tutorial on the Daoist philosopher Zhuangzi, who used to talk about the "wanderings of the truth picker" (采真之遊). This book is about letting the mind wander in the whys of things. Why temple gates needn't have doors, but gardens must always have fences. In these talks, Kathy and I found that the starting point might be something as trivial as the cracks between tatami mats. Wandering on from that, but of course never, ever, stepping on those cracks, we arrived at unexpected conclusions about Japanese society.

What's in these pages doesn't fit in with the history of Japan or Kyoto as usually taught or understood. Much of it is just "lore." It's oral history of a zany sort, because the thoughts are scattered and come from so many random people and places, an anecdote I once heard from a Shinto priest at Oomoto, or a witticism casually dropped by David Kidd.

Much of what I say may turn out not even to be true. Although it should have been. In short, what you will find here is not scholarship, and it's not to be given credit, all my protestations notwithstanding.

At David Kidd's moon-viewing platform in Ashiya (1975)

Gate of Chion-in temple

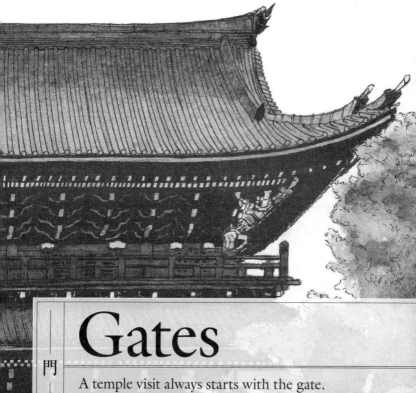

Chapter 1

Gates

門

A temple visit always starts with the gate.
But why are there gates without doors?

hen we go to see one of the temples we've read so much about in the guide-books, we have the temple and its gardens gloriously in our mind's eye as we approach. But when we arrive, what do we see? A gate. No temple in sight.

Thousands of gates, actually I think it might be tens of thousands, are scattered throughout the city. There are grand gates, as high as a three- or four-story building, that tower in front of Chion-in and Nanzenji, and more reserved gates like the thatched "country-style" gate of Honen-in, on down to the modest ones that stand in front of old-style houses. From a street-level point of view, these gates define the city as different. Everywhere else in Japan, it's just a lot of boxy modern buildings. But in Kyoto we have gates. Gates are how we know we're not in Tokyo.

Nowadays the front gate is where tourists queue to buy their entrance tickets. You can see the tide of visitors pooling here before they pass through and surge up the steps to the sight they've come to see. It's a tollbooth.

In the old days, the gate marked much more than that. When people entered the gate, they believed that it made an absolute divide between the outside and inside. At the gate, you reached the end of your journey to get here; and the start of a new, internal journey.

It's a powerful idea that stretches across East Asia, going all the way down to Bali. In Bali, you have these gates which look like a pillar has been cut in half and opened up, leaving the sheer walls of the cut pillar to frame the view of the inside. They're "infinity gates," because there's no upper roof, and no limit to the line of sight. We naturally assume this is the entrance, leading into the temple, but the Balinese see it as an *exit*, taking you out of your daily life.

In Northeast Asia—in China, Korea, and Japan—gates are heavy, roofed structures, the opposite of Balinese emptiness. The Chinese built gates as pavilions, with pillars and roofs, and raised them for greater effect on top of brick and marble pediments. The imposing tiled roofs, with their sweeping rooflines, had an irresistible appeal to builders. So gates got taller and grander, becoming more and more substantial until eventually they turned into buildings in their own right. The Japanese followed this tradition. Larger gates even have worship halls and audience chambers in their upper floors.

You could easily mistake some of the bigger gates for the temples or palaces they give onto. One American friend of mine, who had visited both Tiananmen gate in Beijing and Chion-in gate in Kyoto, was taken aback when he heard me refer to them as "gates." They might have the name "gate" attached to them, but for him, Tiananmen was a palace building, and Chion-in gate was a temple.

Going through a *mon* (gate) came to mean initiation into a religious or artistic secret. On entering you became a disciple of those who dwell beyond the gate. To this day, *monka* (within the gate) or *montei* (younger brothers of the gate) indicate a teacher's disciples; *ichimon* (within one gate) refers to the members of a school or

中华人民共和国万岁　世界人民大团结万岁

Tiananmen gate, Beijing

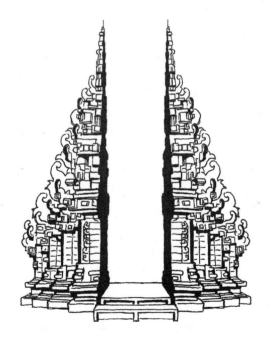

Balinese gate

family. *Hamon* (broken gate) means that someone has been excommunicated or kicked out of a group. And there are dozens of other *mon* words, all referring to the community of people who have passed through a gate.

In Zen, it's still a tradition, at least at Daitokuji, for someone who applies to enter the temple as a disciple to stand outside the gate for three days until a monk comes and admits them. My friend the late John Toler studied Zen at Daitokuji and ultimately became an ordained abbot in Nara. John used to talk of the rigors of that first ordeal. He fainted from thirst and exhaustion. Of course it had all been arranged in advance with the temple that someone would let him in after three days, so he really had nothing to worry about. Decades later, when asked about what it was like studying Zen within Daitokuji, John would always begin with the story of waiting at the gate.

Entering the gate is not something you do lightly. So before going in, let's pause and look at it.

———

The Rule of Three

If it's the gate to a Buddhist temple, it's usually built in three parts. I lived in Kyoto for decades before this simple "Rule of Three" dawned on me. Sometimes the roofs over the middle section are higher, while those over the left and right wings are lower.

But usually they're all sheltered under one roof. In any case, there will be three openings in the gate.

Doing things in threes is deeply satisfying to human beings. It could be as simple as that. Three-part gates are hardly unique to Japan. The Romans used a triple-arch structure for many of their triumphal arches and city gates, Gothic cathedrals featured three-part porticos, and after Palladio it became the standard format for the façade of a Renaissance church. The psychological origins are probably the same.

Once I realized that temple gates were supposed to have three parts, the standard name for them, *sanmon* 三門 (three gates), made sense. I had seen the homonym *sanmon* 山門 (mountain gate) used sometimes for temple gates, and assumed this was the correct version because a temple can also be called a "mountain." But "three gates" turns out to be the original word.

We see plenty of single-entry gates for private residences and palaces. So the Rule of Three would seem to have something to do specially with Buddhism. Monks, who have a lot of free time to think up theories, have come up with ideas to support the Rule of Three. A common one that you hear is the "Three Liberations." The word "Liberation" is a hint that it's got to do with what you leave behind as you enter, that is, it's close to the Balinese idea that the gate is an exit from your normal life. By the way, the three things to be liberated from are "Greed," "Hatred," and "Foolishness."

Doorless Gates

The next thing to note is, does the gate have a door? You can see some with very serious doors, made of thick timbers fitted with metal rivets and huge wooden bolts. The

Roman triumphal triple arch

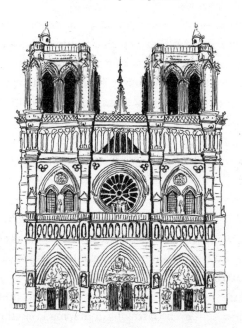

Gothic cathedral three-part portico

most dramatic is at the great gate to Nijo Castle, which was, after all, a fortress. But you'll also find gates with no doors at all. Just airy open spaces between their pillars.

Some of the biggest gates, such as Chion-in and Tofukuji, are completely doorless. This contrasts with the great gates of most other places in the world. Especially all the gates of the Forbidden City in Beijing. They have very solid doors, reinforced with brass studs, built to keep outsiders out and insiders in. I've never seen a discussion anywhere as to why the doorless gate evolved in Japan. But I imagine that, as with so many other things, it's because the Japanese built these gates as symbols, not as real barriers at all.

Once again, the monks have been busy and came up with explanations. I've read that the meaning of a gate without doors is that the Buddhist dharma is open to all comers; that all may enter here freely. Yet plenty of temples have gates that shut and lock. So that logic is a little suspect.

———————

Ah Un

Often only the central entrance opens to allow access. If you look closely, you'll see that while the gate is still designed in three parts, the wings to left and right have been closed off to become boxed-in spaces housing sculptures of guardian deities. For temples these would be *Nio* "guardians," super-muscular hulks standing with arms upraised, eyes glaring, and mouths contorted into a shout or a frown.

Of course, they don't grimace in any old way; there's a rule to those mouths. They're invoking the cosmic sounds *Ah Un*. *Ah* is an open mouth; *Un* is a shut mouth, symbolizing in and out, alpha and omega, sound and silence, the beginning and end of everything.

Ah Un—one side with an open mouth, the other side with a closed mouth—went on from *Nio* guardians to be applied to any protective gate figure. *Shishi* (lions) and *koma-inu* (lion-dogs), found in pairs on either side of a gate, all follow this rule. So do the statues of Heian courtiers carrying quivers of bows and arrows and wearing frizzy hairdos, who take the place of Buddhist *Nio* guardians at Shinto shrines.

While it's a Hindu-Buddhist idea, *Ah Un* went right into Shintoism. The foxes beside the main gate at Fushimi Inari shrine—one with a key in its mouth, the other with a flaming jewel—follow *Ah Un*, as do the other animal sculptures in the Inari grounds.

"Limination"

Actually, there's usually not just one gate as you approach a temple, but a series. It's got to do with the idea of a progression in stages, moving step by step, from the mundane into the holy. Major temple complexes might feature a *nandaimon*, a "great southern gate," so-named because it stood at the foot of the north-south axis along which big temples were aligned. *Nandaimon* are something of a medieval relic you don't see so much in Kyoto, but if you want to see a *nandaimon*, go to Toji temple, which

Top: *Nio* guardians, one with mouth closed, "*Un*," and the other open, "*Ah*"
Bottom: Foxes at Fushimi Inari shrine

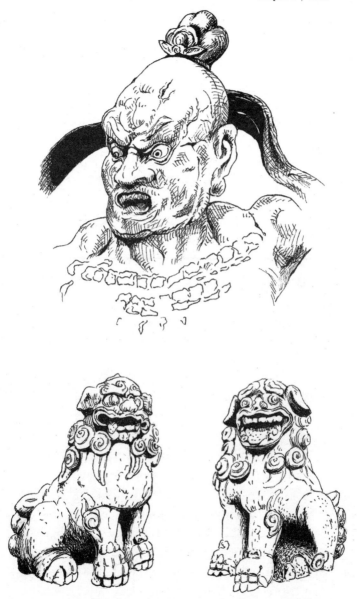

Guardian lion-dogs at Shinto shrine

is one of the few surviving sites dating back to the early 9th century nearly to the founding of the city.

For lesser, or later temples, the series usually starts with a *sanmon*, which is the main gate. If the temple is large enough, there may be more gates before or after this. All of which indicates that you are traveling from the day-to-day into a place special and removed, from lesser to greater mysteries. This comes out of Esoteric Buddhism, where the idea is that you gain enlightenment bit by bit, initiation by initiation.

However, there's another way to look at the lack of doors and the gates lined up in series. It's something that goes to the core of everything Japanese. For this I use the word "limination." Please don't waste time looking it up in a dictionary. I made it up.

It's related to the concept of liminality, a term anthropologists use to describe a threshold, something vague, neither this nor that. Liminality, for the anthropologists, is the condition of being between one state and another—ambiguity at the threshold. I use "limination" to mean exactly the opposite. Limination also signifies a threshold, but in this case a clear-cut one. Doing away with ambiguity. It means drawing lines, arranging things so that discrete spaces are for certain uses, and are separated by barriers from other spaces.

By the way, this runs against the view held by many Japanese concerning their own country: that while the West is clear-cut and precise, Japan is vague and ambiguous. Novelist Oe Kenzaburo even titled his 1994 Nobel Prize acceptance speech, Japan, the Ambiguous, and

Myself. But one could argue that the opposite is true: there are no vague areas, a line is always drawn.

Japan does limination constantly, from defining the seasons (and not just the four seasons, but weekly in the case of flowers for the Tea ceremony), to the floors and ceilings of different parts of a house, down to the edgings between tatami. So a gate can't just be something you happen to walk through on the way from here to there. It must take its place in a "limination sequence." The gate stands at the beginning, or middle, or end, of a walkway.

———————

Axial and Circular Walkways

For many temples and shrines, there's a walkway that begins before you even reach the main gate of the *sanmon*. This is called the *sando* (pilgrimage path). There might be an entry gate at the start of it, and several minor gates along the way. Once inside the main gate, the *sando* continues, and there are more gates.

Sando walkways come in two types: axial and circular. The axial type is found not only at Zen temples but also at large shrines like Kitano Tenmangu. The temple or shrine buildings are aligned along a north-south axis, and the *sando* follows the axis. It may zigzag a bit, but it's basically aligned north-south.

Axial *sando* are the mark of complexes that were planned and built all at one time in one piece, so they follow a system. A thousand years after its founding, the central axis of Toji temple is still clearly visible.

In contrast to Toji's classical design, there's the

circular type of *sando*, like the winding approaches to Kinkakuji and Ryoanji. These came along as afterthoughts, scratched into the grounds of what had been Heian aristocrats' villas, so there's no overall plan. They just meander around the pond and up the hill. That's how you know that these places, although officially Zen temples, don't quite have the seriousness of the others. Once a pleasure palace, always a pleasure palace.

There's a special type of circular walkway, not often seen at temples but which you do encounter at Nijo Castle. It's the helix. You walk through a solid iron-studded gate overlooked by battlements with slatted windows from which they could shoot invaders; and then, what you see in front of you is a flat wall. You have to turn to walk around it, and then veer right to approach the inner gate. It was a defensive stratagem to make it hard for attacking troops to charge straight into the palace.

In contrast, Kyoto and the Chinese-inspired capitals before it, Nara and Asuka, were square grids centered on a north-south axis with gates at the four points of the compass. The most famous gate was Rashomon in the south, which was the city's equivalent of a temple's *nandaimon*. Long before Zen gardens, the old city had its axes and gates. So the axial complexes within the city such as Toji, Myoshinji, the Imperial Palace, and so forth are just repeating on a smaller scale Kyoto's primal plan.

Every once in a while you come across a temple that breaks the mold, and in Kyoto there are two big ones: Higashi-Honganji and Nishi-Honganji, headquarters of the rival sects of True Pure Land Buddhism. Neither one has a *sando*. Both temple complexes border right on a main avenue, so there's no gradual approach. You enter the gate, and you're in the temple grounds, and that's it. These two are unusual for being sited not along the foothills like most of Kyoto's other large temples, but right in the heart of town. Real estate was too precious. So they had to dispense with *sando*.

Another thing that might be a factor in why these two temples have no *sando* is that, before their headquarters moved to Kyoto in the early 17th century, the True Pure Land sects had a history of radical egalitarianism. Their followers built armed citadels, notably in Osaka, from which they fought off warlords and rampaging monks from other sects for centuries. They wanted no part of the tiered levels of enlightenment found in Esoteric or Zen Buddhism. In the True Pure Land sects, all you needed to do was to chant the name of the bodhisattva Amida and you would be saved. So I imagine that when they set up their new headquarters in Kyoto, they felt less need for a series of barriers marking progressive stages of "innerness" and "outerness."

They could do without the *sando* path, but they still felt the need for gates. At Higashi-Honganji they arranged a variety of gates side-by-side inset into the wall facing Karasuma street. It's like a display of gate types carefully selected by a curator. The relatively plain *Genkan-mon* or "entry gate"; the never-opened *Kiku-no-mon* (Chrysanthemum Gate) with its arched roof and big chrysanthemum crest; the grand tripartite *Goeido-mon* with three doors (the tallest temple gate in Japan); and

Array of gates at Higashi-Honganji temple
Left to right: *Amidado-mon*, *Goeido-mon*, *Kiku-no-mon*, *Genkan-mon*

Kiku-no-mon

the arched *Amidado-mon*, roofed with cedar chips. It's an exhibition of gates.

Stairway to Heaven

One item common to *sando*, and especially to the gates, is stairs. One might say, well, so there are stairs. It would hardly seem worth mentioning, but in fact stairways are a big part of visiting a temple. Even if there's not a full flight, there are always a few steps, maybe just three or four, leading up to the gate or carrying on from the gate.

They indicate that you're climbing a mountain. But it's not just any mountain. This mountain has a name, Mount Sumeru. That's the sacred peak at the center of the Hindu and Buddhist universe that the temple stands for. From the Khmer temples of Angkor Wat in Cambodia all the way up to Chinese and Japanese pagodas, each one is a miniature representation of this sacred Mount Sumeru. The gate marks one of the base camps on the way up.

It's a universal rule that one climbs up to a temple. The only exception I can think of is the temple of Sennyuji in southeast Kyoto. The reason must have been that because Sennyuji sits in a little valley they had to build the *sando* in this way. After you climb up to the entry gate, the *sando* swoops downwards into the vale, and there you see, spread out below you, the main hall, and behind it, the walled abbot's quarters. You feel like you've just passed the Himalayas and now you're descending into Shangri-La.

Culture of Stone

Japanese love to say that "Europe is a culture of stone, and Japan is a culture of wood." But Japan too was a culture of stone. Everywhere you go you see stone walls, stone steps, stone tombs, stone Jizo statues, stone stupas, stone monoliths with poems carved into them, stepping stones in gardens, paths with wide flagstones.

The reason these stones pull at the heart lies in how they age. The old way to handle stone carving in Japan was to leave the rock only semi-finished. No perfectly straight edges, no polish and no gloss. These rough-hewn stones then weather with time in Japan's damp mossy climate.

Lichen-covered, chipped and crumbling old steps feel like something that came out of ancient history, out of a time of myth. Japan's primeval mists still swirl around them. That's the cult of Japanese stone. Which makes it all the more remarkable that modern Japanese civil engineering focuses obsessively on the smoothness and whiteness of concrete and granite, on permanence and shine. This ethos has also seeped into temples and shrines, which are now remodeling their *sando* with clean-cut marble. If there is any one area that shows us that Japan's modern culture has turned a corner and truly changed into something else, it is this.

Impressive old stone staircases are still to be found in Kyoto's outskirts, at Kurama in the north and at Kozanji in the west. One of the finest used to be at Jingoji, the temple next to Kozanji, with a legendary flight of mossy steps climbing up to a tall gate. Unfortunately, steep crumbly steps have run afoul of one of Japan's modern obsessions: safety. Even the sides of rice paddies are now lined with shiny protective railings. The steps at Jingoji were seen as dangerous. So like many other old temple steps, they now sport the addition of aluminum banisters right in the middle.

For a wide, steep, truly operatic flight of steps, still without railings, take a look at the stairs leading up to Chion-in gate. Beautiful stairs also remain at Honen-in, where the rough old stones, shaded under spreading branches, set off the thatched gate at the top. The romance of the gate is the romance of the steps.

The concept of a path in stages, with each stage marked by a gate, was taken up in Tea ceremony, which has the *roji* or "dewy path" that you walk through on your way to the tearoom. You pass through the first gate, the *rojimon*, and then you walk a little way until you come to the *chumon* or "middle gate." Beyond the *chumon* lies the inner garden from which you'll step into the tearoom. It removes you step by step from the outer world.

Limination tells you that you are in one spot and it's not the same as what preceded it or what follows. It's a way of creating a flow, a progress, like reading a book. As you pass through a gate, you've turned the page to a new chapter, and at the following gate, you start on the next chapter. Or, you could think of it as unrolling a hand scroll, turning as you go from one image to the next. It's a choreography of space.

———

The Town before the Gate

So far we've stayed inside the temple grounds. Let's step outside for a moment and look back at where we came from. The *sando* leading up to the main gate can stretch quite a way, even into an adjoining neighborhood. The most dramatic example of this happens to be in Omotesando in Tokyo, the avenue lined with fashion houses known as "Japan's Champs-Élysées." Omotesando, "the front *sando*," is the main approach to Meiji shrine. A grand approach like this could be built with modern city planning. The closest to this in Kyoto is the wide road leading to Heian shrine, carved out in the early 1900s by the same nation-building city planners who designed Meiji shrine and its surroundings in Tokyo.

In Kyoto, for older temples and shrines, the growth of the outer *sando* happened more organically. The outer *sando* usually takes the form of a warren of small streets. Called the *monzen machi*, "the town before the gate," this is where the stores, teahouses, restaurants, geisha houses, and souvenir shops congregate. It's where the fun is to be had before you enter the *sanmon* gate and have to give up greed and foolishness. The *monzen machi* of Kiyomizu covers quite a large area, including not only the streets leading up the hill to the temple, but the neighborhood down below near the intersection of Higashiyama-Gojo. It grew into one of Japan's largest ceramics markets, and today it's one of Japan's premier tourist trinket markets. The *monzen machi* of Yasaka shrine became the Gion geisha district.

The two little streets running parallel up to the gate of Chion-in are called Shinmonzen (new town before the gate) and Furumonzen (old town before the gate). Together they make up Chion-in's *monzen machi*, and they've become Kyoto's antiques district. This is where I've left behind much of my greed and foolishness.

Grand and Humble Gates

From the *monzen machi*, let's return to gates. So far we've looked at them from the point of view of religious symbolism—the way they divide the mundane world from the sacred in a series of stages. But there's another aspect to gates, which is status—the way they tell us about the power and position of the owner of the gate.

In the Edo period, the Shogunate was much concerned that people live according to their proper class. To make sure that people kept to their assigned place in life, the Shogunate issued *ken'yakurei* (sumptuary laws) defining what clothes people could wear, the sort of houses they could build, and so forth. For example, they decreed that peasants should only wear simple and modest fabrics such as indigo; the houses of merchants should not have carved decorations. Gates came in for quite a bit of attention in these laws. Commoners couldn't have certain kinds of gates without special permission. Samurai and temples, too, had gates prescribed by their status.

So the gate is telling you who's who. If you see a two-story gate with battlements, that's a "castle gate" or *yagura-mon*. The two-story gate of Omotesenke Tea

Headquarters was a gift from the Tokugawa daimyo of Kishu, whose noble family supported Omotesenke during the later years of the Shogunate. It lets us know that the Grand Master of Omotesenke Tea, while not quite a samurai, was seen to hold a rank equivalent to a high lord.

Urasenke Tea's much simpler *kabuto-mon* (helmet gate) tells a more complex tale. The gate, thatched with cedar chips, was copied from the *kabuto-mon* in the grounds of Ryoko-in, a subtemple of Daitokuji. That gate in turn was said to have once been the gate of Sen no Rikyu, the founder of Tea.

Foreign writers, when they introduce this gate, seem to be much impressed by its "simplicity," and "humbleness." But people of an earlier era would have known, first of all, that the gate harkened back to the time when Rikyu lived in a lavish palace as Hideyoshi's neighbor at Jurakudai; and secondly, thatched or not, the helmet shape was forbidden for commoners. By its shape, the *kabuto-mon* in fact proclaims wealth and status, and does it as effectively as the wrought-iron gates of a Beverly Hills mansion.

At the same time, there is a touch of humbleness after all. Urasenke, the most junior branch of the three Sen hereditary families of Tea ceremony, has a single-story gate, thatched with cedar. So the Ura gate is suitably more modest than the two-story ceramic-tiled daimyo battlement of the senior Omote family. By their gates thou shalt know them.

As in the case of my friend who thought that the Chion-in gate was the temple itself, the gate can sometimes be the part of a temple complex that makes the deepest impression. The multi-gabled gate of Chion-in, raised high on a steep set of wide steps, is one of the grandest structures in the country. Its spectacular roof-lines are always a joy to see, even when just driving by. Climb up the steps beyond the gate, and you reach a wide clearing in the middle of which stands the enormous temple of Chion-in. Although massive, it leaves so little impact on most visitors that they can barely recall it. The gate is what remains in everybody's memory.

Honen-in came up earlier for its combination of gate and steps. Consecrated to Honen, one of the early founders of Pure Land Buddhism, its rustic thatched gate tells us that this is not a "major" temple (it was established as a meditation retreat by much larger Chion-in). It began as a hermitage, and the gate is like a sign saying this.

The thatched gate is charming in any season—whether deep in the greenery of spring or summer, or in the autumn when ruby-red maple leaves have fallen onto the thatch, or in winter when snow has covered the little stairway leading up to it. The gate gives the temple the feeling of a hideaway and a sage's retreat. Once you have gone through that gate, even though there are splendid features like raised sand gardens and historic structures inside, it is still the gate that is the temple's truest secret. For connoisseurs of Kyoto's gates, Honen-in takes first place.

―――――

Imperial Gates

At the other end of the spectrum from Honen-in's low-key thatched gate, the more important temples will

Omotesenke's *yagura-mon* gate

Urasenke's *kabuto-mon* gate

sometimes feature an opulent *karamon*, a so-called "Chinese gate" with an arched roof in the center. *Kara* means Chinese, but to the best of my knowledge, nothing like these gates has ever existed in China. I don't know what's so "Chinese" about them. Perhaps they were called *kara* because Chinese things were thought to be gorgeous.

The rounded roof shape is known as *karahafu* (projecting Chinese roof), and you often see roofs like this added as a decorative touch to the eaves of palaces, temples, and shrines. In Japan, the land of straight lines and sharp angles, their roundness stands out. Come to think of it, it's the roundness that might have made people feel something foreign and un-Japanese in them. In any case, *karahafu* roofs appeared early from Heian onwards, and seem to have denoted high rank. You find them on castles and prestigious temples and shrines. When such a roof crowns a gate, the gate becomes a *karamon*, signifying the highest status of all—Imperial connections.

One of the most stunning of the *karamon* is at Nijo Castle and there's another at Nishi-Honganji. It's called *Higurashi-no-mon* (The Gate at the End of the Day) because, covered with gilded carvings, it's so beautiful that a viewer will become lost in admiring it and forget that the end of the day has come.

Karahafu roofs, being of high status, are often used for *chokushi-mon* (the gate of the Imperial Emissary). These feature elaborate bronze fittings and doors of wooden filigree with chrysanthemum crests carved into them. And they are never opened. Ever. *Chokushi* is the Imperial Emissary who arrives from the court to take part

Rustic Honen-in gate

in certain ceremonies. But except for some very special temples, at very few times of the year—or maybe just once in a reign—such emissaries are extremely rare. These days they are almost non-existent, but the gates still stand by the dozen within the grounds of Kyoto temples.

Because the emissary never comes, the gate is always closed. Often the *chokushi-mon* is in a garden, where it may not have been opened for hundreds of years. There's one that stands in the garden of Sanbo-in at Daigoji temple in Yamashina. It has Japan's earliest daimyo strolling garden, built by Hideyoshi, and that beautiful *chokushi-mon* is the centerpiece of the garden. You'll see one at Nanzenji, Myoshinji, and many a subtemple of Daitokuji.

In the Zen subtemples, the *chokushi-mon* might be set into a wall at the back of a sand garden. There's no pathway to it; you'd have to trudge through raked sand and tromp over landscaped moss to get to the gate. Which indicates that nobody's expecting it to be opened any time soon.

My favorite *chokushi-mon* is the one at Joshokoji, an ancient countrified Zen temple in the far northwest of Kyoto. It stands on a slight rise, approached by a flight of diagonal steps, among the more unusual stairs in Kyoto. Did an emissary ever come here? Maybe four hundred years ago? If he did, I wonder how he scuttled sideways up those diagonal steps. Anyway, the gate still stands there proudly, demonstrating that this quiet little retreat in the hills is not just a country temple, but was built by an Emperor.

Karamon gate at Nijo Castle

Gates without Walls

David Kidd, who came to Japan via China and tended to view everything through a Chinese lens, told me that when he first arrived in Japan he was disturbed to find that gates in Japan don't always have accompanying walls, or much of a wall. Some of the most important gates stand there in complete isolation, such as the main gate of Daitokuji, or the National Treasure gate of Tofukuji.

Being so imbued with China, David found this strange because Chinese walls are enormous. They can be twenty-foot-thick, towering structures with "real" gates that are bolted shut at a certain hour, and you can't go freely in and out of these compounds unless you pass through the gate.

I once got locked in one of the Ming Tombs outside of Beijing because I stayed too late. I was walking the circuit of the inner wall with my friend Mrs. Wang, and by the time we got back out to the gate everything had been locked up. It happened to be January, twenty degrees below zero, the caretaker had left, and we could not climb out because the walls are thirty feet high. It was very scary, but I'll save the story of how I got out for another time.

In Japan that wouldn't be a problem because you could easily just walk out. At Nanzenji, one of the most important gates in Japan, there's no wall at all. It just stands there. David found this idea of gates as freestanding structures rather absurd, and wondered what was the point of gates you could just walk around.

A dramatic example of a wall-less gate is the *Niomon* of Kiyomizu temple, so-called because it houses two *Nio* guardian statues in the boxed-off wings to the side of the entrance. (Of course they grimace *Ah* and *Un*.) Restored in 2003 and painted a brilliant vermillion, the gate is surrounded by a gleaming expanse of white granite. Glowing psychedelically against a blue summer sky, the gate stands marooned amidst the granite like a solitary electric pole in the middle of a parking lot.

═══════════

Torii

Gates standing wide open without doors, and devoid of walls, so you could just walk around them if you wanted to. The *chokushi-mon* that never open, waiting centuries for an emissary who will never come. It's got to do with the symbolism of "gate-hood," and not reality.

To take the open gate to its furthest degree, you have the torii, the gate to a Shinto shrine that is barely three-dimensional; one can draw it with a few lines. With the torii the Japanese departed from the Chinese model of a substantial roofed gate functioning as a building in its own right. They reduced the gate to two dimensions. Torii gates are pure symbols.

Torii stand there naked in the middle of a space and merely inform you that beyond this spot is a sacred place. Remarkably, it works. Torii have psychic power. The one torii that for many people symbolizes the city is the great gate of Heian shrine. While it belongs to Heian shrine, of course, it almost feels like the gate to the city itself.

The great torii of Heian shrine

Rows of torii at Fushimi Inari shrine

Torii come in many different types. There's the simple style, just two columns with a beam across the top and a crossbeam below that. More common is the type of torii as at Heian shrine where the top beam has a Chinese

Torii with pyramidal top at Hiyoshi Taisha shrine

touch, with a slight upward flare at the ends. Torii can be wood, stone or concrete, bronze-clad, and very often painted red. Most distinctive are the torii of Hiyoshi Taisha and its associated Hie and Sanno shrines across the country that have a pyramid-like crown on top of the torii, a relic of Hiyoshi shrine's ancient relationship with the great Esoteric Buddhist temple on Mount Hiei.

At Fushimi Inari shrine, the bright red torii proliferated, swallowing up the *sando* walkway, and marching up the hillside behind. It's a hallucinogenic efflorescence of torii gates. There is of course a big Shinto shrine at Fushimi Inari, and it's very important because it's the head shrine of the Inari cult. But most people hardly give the shrine a passing glance. They walk behind it, where they can see the thousands of red torii lined up on paths that climb the hills above the shrine. You can walk for hours without passing under the same torii twice. At the small altars scattered along the hillside you'll find piled up, as offerings, miniature torii of all sizes. It's the ultimate gate-themed landscape.

———————

Hidden Chambers

So far we've only talked about the outer look and symbolism of Kyoto's gates. Many have interiors too. One well-kept secret of Kyoto is that the larger gates feature on their second floors great tableaux of paintings and sculptures—a coiling dragon painted in green, orange, red, and blue glares down from the center of the ceiling; the beams writhe with mythical birds and winged angels. Against the back wall, on a raised altar, sits a haloed statue of the Buddha, attended by a row of sculptures of *rakan*, "perfected beings." Big-headed, bug-eyed, with comical moustaches and twisting arms and legs, each *rakan* is more eccentric than the next. The whole is finished off with chunks of driftwood.

This is what you will see if you gain entry to the second floors of the gates at Daitokuji, Chion-in, Tofukuji, and Nanzenji. Some of Japan's best ceiling paintings are found in these gates. In the case of Daitokuji, the frescoes were done by the great genius of early Edo painting, Hasegawa Tohaku, so they're among the more precious art works in the country.

A lot of expense and artistic effort went into the paintings and sculptures in the upper rooms of these gates. But except for a few select monks who might perform a ritual up there now and then, these masterpieces were not intended to be seen by human eyes. The purpose of these gaudily decorated chambers was protective. They were semi-secret places, never open to the public, like the crypts or treasuries of European cathedrals.

At ground level, the public shuffles through the gates, unaware that rooms of heavenly splendor are spread out in the gloomy chambers just over their heads. It used to be that those upstairs rooms were forever hidden. You could live for decades in Kyoto and never see one. But recently, temples have started opening them up as part of the seasonal tourist campaigns, and if you're lucky, one of the gates' upper stories will be open for viewing somewhere.

It's time to enter the gate. But before we do so, we have to look again, because David Kidd was wrong. There are walls. There are lots of walls.

Tiled-roofed wall with white stripes,
Imperial Palace

Chapter 2

Walls

塀

Temple and palace walls grew out of a Buddhist concept of the wall that protects from primal chaos.

hile big gates may stand alone, there is in fact no lack of walls. We just hadn't been looking for them. There will be a wall around the temple somewhere, before or behind the great gate. Walls have a symbolism that's even older than Buddhist gates.

This brings us to the larger reason why gates and walls matter. Asian temples and shrines are not "one thing." At Notre Dame or Chartres Cathedral, a single great monument stands there by itself. But temples like Kiyomizu are part of a "complex"—gates, walls, walkways, corridors, worship halls, and pagodas. There are also drum and bell towers, minor shrines, and the residences of monks and priests.

What part of all this is the "temple" you've come to see? Sometimes, as with the Golden Pavilion, shining majestically all by itself at the side of a pond, you can be sure that this is important, and the smattering of other structures in the temple precincts doesn't really matter. But with the Silver Pavilion, which is just a dull wooden shack pushed over to the side of the complex, it's not so clear. In fact, very little of what attracts people to the Silver Pavilion is found in the pavilion itself. Its appeal lies in the tall-hedged walkway leading up to it, in the gardens, in the abbot's hall, in the big sand mound. In the "complex."

The Cosmic Wall
The temple complex is found from Indonesia and

Thailand all the way up through China and over to Japan. The name for this, *garan*, is very old, derived from ancient Sanskrit. The earliest form of the *garan* was strict and axial, modeled after Indian temples and Chinese palaces. In Nara, you'll find the more classic form with everything balanced neatly left and right and a roofed cloister surrounding the inner courtyard. Once you get into the Heian period, the *garan* becomes looser, more free-form; temples dispense with the cloister, and the pieces of the *garan* get scattered around a bit. It's tempting to see in this the Japanese tendency to bring a bit of creative anarchy to the perfect original.

The concept of a *garan* arises from Hindu cosmology, according to which the universe centers around a mountain called Mount Sumeru. Sometimes it's called Mount Meru instead of Sumeru. It's the peak on which the Lord of the Universe, Indra, sits. As we saw earlier with the steps leading up to temples, every temple is a symbolic Mount Sumeru.

In the ancient cosmology, Sumeru is surrounded by lesser mountain peaks, each inhabited by gods, like condominiums in which higher-status deities dwell on the upper floors. Enclosing these peaks is the Cosmic Wall, which separates it all from the sea of chaos in which the universe exists.

━━━━━━━

Quincunx

What I've just described is the "quincunx" design of 12th century Angkor Wat with its moat and wall. Quincunx

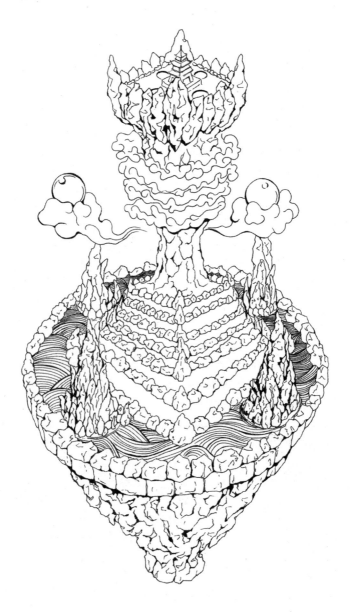

Mount Sumeru encircled by the "Cosmic Wall"

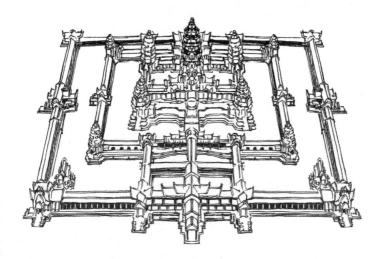

Angkor Wat "quincunx" layout

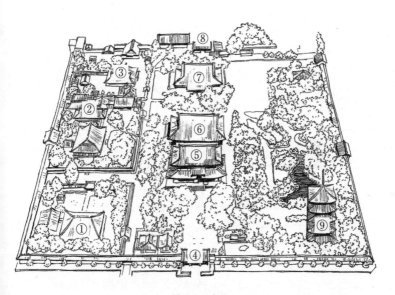

Toji complex
① Kanjo-in, ② Shoin and Kyakuden reception halls, ③ Kobo Daishi commemorative hall,
④ *Nandaimon* south gate, ⑤ Kondo worship hall, ⑥ Kodo lecture hall, ⑦ dining hall,
⑧ *Kitadaimon* north gate, ⑨ five-level pagoda

is a rare and wonderful old English word that I've loved since first hearing about it as a high-school student, a term coined by Sir Thomas Browne. A quincunx is an arrangement of five points like five dots on a dice; one each at the four corners of a square, and one in the center. Angkor Wat, once a Hindu and later a Buddhist temple complex, is a quincunx because it has four lower towers and one tall one in the center representing Mount Sumeru.

In Japanese, the word for Mount Sumeru is *Shumisen*. Statues of the Buddha sit on a pedestal called the *shumidan* or "Altar of Mount Sumeru." It usually tapers in the middle to signify a rising mountain, widening at the top like a high plateau. On this platform sits the Buddha, having taken the place of Indra. The temple encloses this Mount Sumeru arrangement like those black lacquer cases that used to house Buddhist statues. You could say that the temple is "the box that Mount Sumeru comes in."

The pagodas and gates within a Kyoto temple complex take the place of Angkorian towers. They're the outer points of a quincunx. This being Japan, and not China or the Khmer empire at Angkor, the emphasis was on the *concept* of a quincunx, not a real one. There might be three towers instead of four, and any number of entry gates in the surrounding walls. The quincunx isn't exact; the main temple might be a bit right or left of the axis. It's gone a bit off kilter.

The Japanese variant on the quincunx is a complex of seven, rather than five, parts. Maybe I should coin a new word; we could call it a "septunx." This is called a *shichido garan* (seven-hall *garan*) and it was seen as ideal. As to just what the seven halls should be, experts disagree. Temples will proudly proclaim that they're fully outfitted as a *shichido garan*, but when you ask what the seven parts are, opinions vary.

They don't seem to have followed a hard and fast rule. There would usually be the *sanmon* (gate), the *kondo* (worship hall), the *kodo* (lecture hall), the *to* (pagoda), a *kyozo* (sutra repository), plus a drum tower and a bell tower. Depending on the sect, there might be a *zendo* (meditation hall), a *Goeido* (founder's hall), *kuri* (monks' residence), *hojo* (abbot's residence), a *tahoto* (pagoda with round upper floor), and so forth. In actual fact, a temple doesn't need to have seven halls or towers to be called a *shichido garan*. It could be any number; the word has come to mean simply "a great and complete Buddhist complex."

Whatever type of "unx" it may be, the temple complex symbolizes the mountain at the center of the world. That's why temples are commonly called "mountains." Depending on their sect, important temples that control branches in other places might describe themselves as *Honzan* (main mountain) and if their sect boasts a lot of subsidiaries (these can number in the hundreds, or even thousands), they might be called *Dai-honzan* (great main mountain). Even a small temple is still a mountain, and so you always find steps and staircases to go along with the gates. You're climbing up to Mount Sumeru.

And around all this, you will always find the Cosmic Wall.

Letting Walls Fall Where They May

Walls in Japan became the focus of a great deal of ingenuity. Builders didn't construct the thick, high walls that you would see in China. There's nothing in Kyoto even remotely as impressive as the vast red towering walls that encircle Beijing's Forbidden City. But when you think of the principle of "limination" at work, and all the emphasis on fine points of status and moving in stages from lower to higher, it's natural that the Japanese would come up with a wide variety of walls.

First of all, there's the angle of slope. Walls are an exception to the rule—applying to almost everything else in Japan—that manmade things must follow ninety-degree angles. Think of Japanese architecture and what comes to mind is arrangements of squares and rectangles. That's what so impressed the German architectural critic Bruno Taut in the 1930s when he visited Katsura Detached Palace. Those neat right angles were such a relief after the curlicues and filigree of Baroque and Victorian architecture in Europe.

In contrast with Japan, in Thailand everything is a trapezoid—windows, gates, doors, walls—they all taper at the top, there's never a ninety-degree angle. Thai builders avoided it at all costs. They even bowed the bases of temples downwards to exaggerate the slanting effect even more.

In China, you find a lot of curves: moon gates, round windows, circular walls, even round buildings such as the famous main hall of the Temple of Heaven in Beijing.

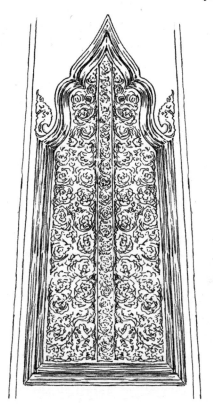

Trapezoidal Thai window

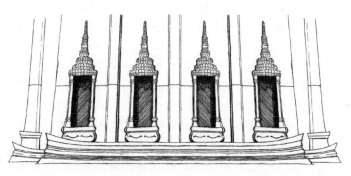

Sloping base and slanting columns of Thai temple

In Japan, they frowned on curves. Buildings might zigzag, but they rarely bend. I wonder if it arose from the culture of all-wooden buildings, where fitting beams and pillars together at right angles came naturally.

However, the rule of right angles and straight lines doesn't apply to stone walls. The larger walls in Japan do curve outwards, and the line of those curves is one of the most beautiful things in the country. Think of the ramparts of Nijo Castle resting on a broad concave stone base. This shape gives these walls their strength in earthquakes. It's a natural way to build a wall to be stronger, and it has an inherent beauty because the curvature of that line reflects the pull of the earth.

There's an English name for the curved line that supports castle walls. That particular slope that's steeper at the top and flares outward at the base is called a "catenary." It's nature's way of supporting a constant force. For example, think of the cables that swoop downward from a suspension bridge's towers, or the sloping chain leading from a boat to its anchor. Those things are catenaries. It's the ideal line of stress that allows the anchor to hold the boat, cables to hold the bridge, and of course, the walls of the castle not to come tumbling down.

The catenary is a natural and mathematically sound curve for structural engineering, and yet for some reason, nobody used it but Japan. Not even the mathematically inclined West ever built walls with a catenary slope. One can only guess why. Perhaps, in China and Europe, a flat surface at a fixed angle seemed to have more finesse and therefore appealed to the engineers of empire. The

Nijo Castle walls

Catenary slope of cables on Akashi Kaikyo bridge

catenary—just letting the walls "fall where they may"—might have seemed a lazy solution. In fact, it was the most efficient. In any case, this is what accounts for the elegant look of the walls and moats of Nijo Castle and all the other Japanese castles.

———————

Entasis

Important temple walls, too, rise if not at a catenary slope, at least at a slant from a broader base. It's an obvious way to make a wall more stable. But there's also something about that shape that's very satisfying. I think the reason that the Thais fell in love with the trapezoid was that it creates an illusion of height, like the "entasis" of Greek columns. When you look at a Greek temple, the columns appear perfectly straight, but actually they're designed so that they bulge in the middle and taper at the top. They called this entasis; a trick of perspective. A thing with sides that rise at right angles will look a bit squat, but make it so that it's smaller at the top than at the bottom, and it has a slimmer, more graceful look.

This was well understood by the 17th century warlord and tea master Kobori Enshu, who designed the shape of *andon* (floor lamps). An Enshu *andon* was basically a lantern in the shape of a tube. Standing about sixty centimeters tall and thirty centimeters in diameter, it was made of paper stretched around four vertical pieces of wood, resting on a round base and with a wooden ring at the top. Inside would be a candle or a dish holding oil and a wick.

Trapezoidal wall

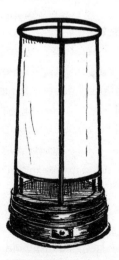

Andon floor lamp

An *andon* looks like a tube, but actually it's a cone. The top is slightly narrower than the bottom. The sides make a trapezoid, and that slight entasis gives the *andon* a graceful feel. They once stood by the millions in every house and temple, but you seldom see *andon* in Japan these days. Few Japanese are even familiar with the word. I saw my first ones in David Kidd's palace years ago, and ever since have been collecting antique *andon*. Every house I've restored has them. They're my trademark. I can't live without them. All because of that little bit of *entasis.*

Japan applied the trick of entasis to walls. A two- or three-meter wall, built perfectly straight, would look "heavy," whereas if it slopes a bit it takes on a kind of lightness. If it's a very big wall, it will slope outwards in a catenary; if it is a smaller wall, it will slant like a trapezoid.

Of Kyoto's "high classic" walls, the most beautiful is probably the stately one bounding the southern edge of Toji temple. It rises from a grassy mound bordered by a moat, with walls sloping with a pronounced trapezoidal slant. A truly fine roof with old-fashioned tubular tiles, nicer than the tiled roofs on most houses, runs all along the top of the wall.

You'll find similar trapezoidal walls of this "classic" type at Nijo Castle, Chishaku-in, and other important temples, as well as in the grounds of the Imperial Palace.

═══════════

Roofs on Walls

Another thing, the biggest difference between walls in East Asia and walls in the West, is that they have roofs.

You find this a lot in China and very much in Japan. Actually, it's not only walls; every vertical structure has a roof—wells, bridge beams, even signboards. Each one of the dozens of crossbeams making up the stilted frame-work that the verandah of Kiyomizu rests on has its own little protective roof.

There will often be a little roof on top of a bamboo fence. On a plaster wall, usually the roof would be tiles, but sometimes you even find thatch.

One would assume that roofs on walls are simply a way to shelter them from rain, but I wonder. England and France had plenty of rain, but they didn't do this. Maybe it came from China's penchant for creating end-less replicas of the Forbidden City. The roofs give us the feeling that these aren't just walls or fences; they're more like compressed buildings, like a colonnade or a cloister that's been flattened into two dimensions.

Combine the elegance of the narrowing trapezoid of the walls with the roof on the top, and a structure that's just a barrier between here and there becomes graceful in its own right. It's like the Gothic windows of the palaz-zos of Venice. Think of the Grand Canal, and what you see in your mind is those exquisite windows. It's the same with the walls of Kyoto.

―――――――

The Stones of Kyoto
Another thing that you often see in walls is what I call the "smooth-rough boundary." One trait of Japanese archi-tecture is the sudden contrast between flat, manmade

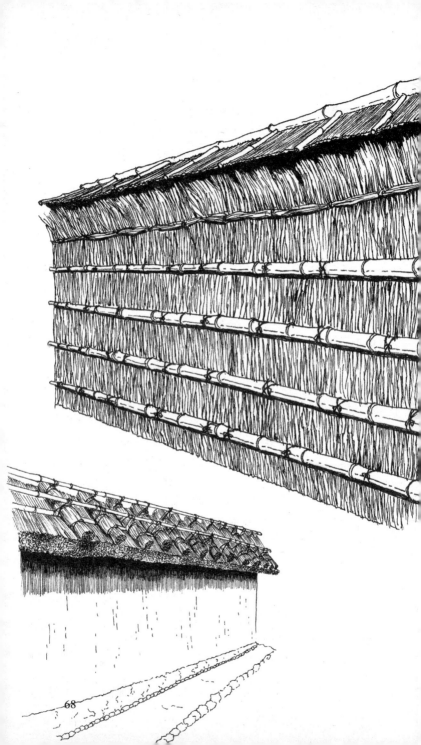

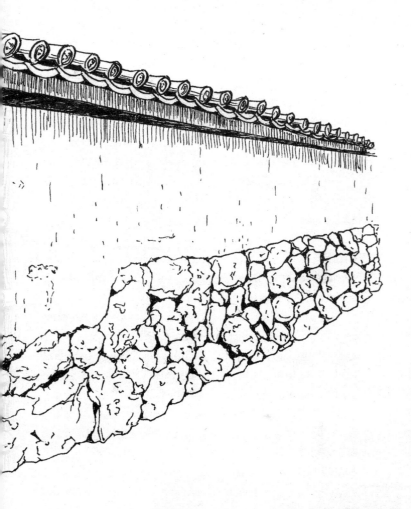

Top left: Bamboo and rush fence roofed with wooden boards and bamboo
Left: Thatch-roofed wall
Above: Wall with smooth plaster surface on rough stone base

surfaces and coarse natural textures. In the lower part of a *minka* (old Japanese house), everything up to head level and a few feet above is flat wood surfaces; but when you get above that you find big pieces of raw lumber.

The smooth-rough boundary especially applies to walls. If you look at a typical Japanese wall, you see an upper plane of smooth plaster, descending to a base made of rough stones. The stones are sometimes flattened but very often not. They're basically just a row of boulders. The plaster fits into and rises from the interstices of that line of rocks. This is quite unlike a Western or even a Chinese wall where the wall would rest on a perfectly straight base. In Japan, you go from this smooth plaster surface straight to rough stones.

For a lover of rough stones—not just the fancy ones they place in gardens, but the weightier ones used for castle foundations—there are none better than the giant rocks making up the wall that fronts Toyokuni shrine and Hokoji temple, just north of the Kyoto National Museum. This wall is one of the few remnants of Hideyoshi's extravagant building binge in the late 1500s. His Jurakudai Castle was the first castle with stone walls to be built in Kyoto. It stood north of present-day Nijo Castle, but was three times larger than Nijo. Hideyoshi had every surface covered with gold right down to the roof tiles. We know it's not just a legend from the amazed accounts of Jesuit visitors of the time—Jurakudai really was gold-covered. Every once in a while they dig up some of the gold-leafed roof tiles. This golden monument didn't last long though. Hideyoshi ordered it dismantled in a fit of megalomaniacal pique only nine years after it was built.

Hideyoshi's equally massive temple of Hokoji has also vanished. It covered grounds that now encompass Toyokuni shrine, the small Hokoji temple that still exists today, the National Museum, and several other nearby temple grounds. Hideyoshi's Hokoji temple stood taller than Osaka Castle, and covered an area double the size of Nara's Todaiji. With the fall of the Toyotomi dynasty after Hideyoshi's death, most of the lands were confiscated. In later centuries Hokoji burned down again and again, each time being rebuilt a little smaller (the last fire was in 1973), until today only a rather modest Buddha sits inside tiny Hokoji temple. What remains of the lost grandeur is this row of giant stones.

Kyoto people call these "crying stones," although it's not clear if it's just one stone or all of them that are crying. Some say they weigh enough to make one cry; others that the feudal lords who were forced by Hideyoshi to transport these stones from far away cried at the great expense of it all.

For a connoisseur of stone battlements, another choice remnant of Hideyoshi's era is to be found in a pile of stones in a shrine in southern Kyoto. They are relics of Kohatayama Fushimi Castle, Hideyoshi's grandest monument in Kyoto, the last of the hundred castles he built in his lifetime. Built on a hill southeast of the capital, it was larger than Jurakudai Castle and Hokoji temple combined. The hill on which it stood, called Momoyama, has given us the name of the era (from the late 16th century to the early 17th century), synonymous with golden magnificence.

Within a few decades of Hideyoshi's death, the Tokugawa shoguns had dismantled it all. They donated bits and pieces to temples and shrines. Fragments of it can be found all over the city, such as the library at Daigoji, the *karamon* gate at Nishi-Honganji, Hiunkaku (Flying Cloud Pavilion), also at Nishi-Honganji, and so forth. Hideyoshi's widow Nene was allowed to take the tearooms Kasa-tei and Shigure-tei with her to her retirement villa that later became Kodaiji temple.

The stone walls, however, were military, dangerous reminders of the great lord whom the Tokugawas had supplanted. So they went to almost as much trouble demolishing the walls down to the last block as it took to build the castle in the first place. All that's left is a pile of stones in the grounds of Gokonomiya Jinja, a little shrine tucked away near Momoyama Goryomae station. We've gone from Momoyama splendor to no trace of a wall. Just a jumble of rocks.

Wall Palette

One thing typical of Japan is to embellish a simple concept, coming up with all sorts of alternate versions. Themes and variations. And so they played with color.

In Beijing, vivid red walls surround the Forbidden City and all the palaces inside. In Southern China, walls will often be a deep ochre yellow. Japan as a rule avoided strong colors; here the walls are mostly done in white, but also in pale pastel shades of yellow, orange, gray, or green. But there are exceptions. Sometimes you see an all-black wall, such as surrounded David Kidd's second house, the one he moved to in his later years in Kyoto. David used to say, "The ominous black is because the house once belonged to a powerful moneylender." Then there are the pinkish red walls of Ichiriki geisha teahouse in Gion, typical of the pleasure districts. Red and pink are the colors of a particular occupation—geisha.

The white or pale pastels of most walls would not seem to allow for a strong visual appeal, but there are ways to create intriguing surface effects on plaster. In Nara's Horyuji temple, builders built up the walls gradually by pressing one layer of clay after another between wooden boards. This was to make the walls stronger. Over the years the surface has worn away, giving them a layered look, almost like weathered wood.

In Kyoto, the most famous example of this process can be found in the wall around the Ryoanji garden. The wood grain effect is further accentuated by the use of clay that was kneaded in oil. With the passage of time the oil has seeped through to the surface, creating a marbled pattern of browns, grays, yellows, and blacks.

Actually Ryoanji garden really needs these walls. Without them, the impression is bleak; the garden verges on sterility. The walls add a sense of something aged and organic. They bring life to the place.

Another thing that you will see around Kyoto city—it's typical of the life of the townspeople—is that the lower half of the wall is surfaced with wooden planks.

This is to protect against rain wearing away the lower wall, and in the past, against mud splattered by passing carts and so forth. The lower wooden paneling can be either rough-grained *sugi* (cedar) or *yakisugi* (charred cedar). The few feet of dark wood creates a band of black below the white plaster of the wall.

Recycled Walls

White stripes running horizontally along a wall's surface signify high status. You'll find them at dozens of temples in Kyoto, especially *monzeki jiin*, temples at which an Imperial family member once served as abbot. They're also to be seen at the Imperial Palace and Nijo Castle. In Edo days you needed special permission from the Shogunate to plaster a wall with white stripes. It's said that there were walls with three, four, or five stripes depending on the temple's place in the hierarchy, but over time "stripe inflation" set in, and today you can mostly find walls with five stripes or more.

Sometimes to give strength to the mud or the plaster, builders inset clay tiles into the wall to make these stripes. As you drive south down Kawaramachi, you can see the mud-tile-mud effect in the wall enclosing Shosei-en, the huge detached garden of Higashi-Honganji. Although it takes up a square block of the central city, most people aren't even aware that it's there. Only the wall suggests that something important lies inside.

It's worth taking a walk along this wall, especially the eastern side that faces Kawaramachi road. It must be

Patterned earthen wall at Ryoanji

one of Kyoto's longest continuous walls, and as you walk you see a changing display of tiles, some old and broken, some new and fresh, inset into stretches of orange, yellow, and gray plaster. The oldest part consists of broken tiles, and while no historical records survive, one theory has it that these are the remains of the buildings that stood in the old garden before it was destroyed in 1864 by a fire.

The fire occurred at the very end of the Edo period, in the struggles leading up to the Meiji Restoration of 1868. It began with a clash between royalists and Edo Shogunate troops at the *Hamaguri-gomon* (Clam Gate) of the palace in what's known popularly as the "Clam Gate Rebellion." The flames spread quickly, eventually wiping out nearly 30,000 homes and temples in the center of the city, including Shosei-en. This fire marked the boundary between old Edo-era Kyoto and the new Meiji Kyoto that rose on its ashes.

According to the "recycled debris" theory, it's believed that when they rebuilt the villa in the 1860s and 1870s, they recycled old stones and tiles remaining from the disaster. As we saw, smaller broken tiles feature in the outer wall along Kawaramachi. Larger pieces—rocks that had been part of walls and foundations, pillars, grinding stones—were gathered up and put together into a collage, making Kyoto's most striking wall of all, the so-called "High Stones" inside the villa.

The High Stones wall of Shosei-en is first of all, of course, a wall, a big one proclaiming the prestige of Higashi-Honganji. At the same time, it's a self-conscious

Outer wall of Shosei-en villa inset with old tiles

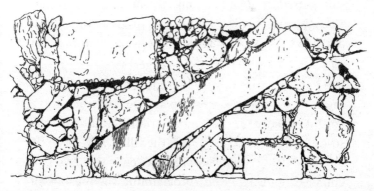

The "High Stones" of Shosei-en villa

art work. One can imagine it appearing as an installation at a contemporary art museum, labeled *Destruction and Reconstruction #5*.

The High Stones wall exemplifies a typical post-Meiji trend, which is the use of bits and pieces of the past as accents in modern gardens. Once the world of old Japan had vanished, it was time to recycle the fragments. The celebrated garden designer of the 20th century, Shigemori Mirei, would often reuse pillar bases in his creations, notably in his "Big Dipper" garden (1939) at Tofukuji. In the middle of an expanse of streaked white sand, he placed seven stone pillar supports that were found when they restored one of the old temple structures.

You will also see pillar bases like this in many a tea garden. When we're told, for example, that the central stone in a certain garden came from Hideyoshi's vanished Jurakudai palace, it creates a link to the past, reminding us of Kyoto's many layers of history. The crying stones at Hokoji wall, the pieces of castle ramparts gathered up and preserved at Gokonomiya shrine, the outer wall of Shosei-en inset with broken tiles, and the High Stones wall made from a collage of architectural fragments—all of these are Kyoto referring back to itself.

Wall Experiences

For a full wall experience, there's nothing better than the labyrinthine Myoshinji compound. Like many Zen temples, Myoshinji is "collegiate," in that it grew up much in

"Big Dipper" garden, by Shigemori Mirei, Tofukuji temple

the same way as Oxford or Cambridge. At Oxford, there are central facilities such as the museum and the library. But ninety percent of the university grounds is taken up by the colleges—some larger some smaller, some new and some very old—in which the teaching, dining, and most other activities take place.

Likewise at a collegiate temple (Daitokuji is another one), you have a central meditation hall, a lecture hall, the chief abbot's residence, and some other shared buildings. The rest of the complex is made up of independent subtemples, each with its own gates, chapels, and gardens. As at Oxford, some are rich, others less so. Some have low-key moss gardens going back to Muromachi, and others have dramatic piles of sculpturesque gravel concocted by modern garden designers. Most are closed to the public, but a few are open. Each subtemple is different, but one thing they have in common is walls.

This makes a compound like Myoshinji into a miniature city-within-a-city, with avenues, side streets, and dozens of walls and gates. You can wander around the lanes for hours just as you can inside Beijing's Forbidden City. Some walls are higher and some lower. Some are white and some are yellow with white stripes. At a certain time in late afternoon, the pine trees cast their shadows onto the plaster, and you can see silhouetted every twig and pine needle. It looks just like an ink painting of a pine tree done in pale gray ink-wash. If you want to understand why ink paintings look the way they do, there's no better way than to spend an afternoon at Myoshinji.

On the street side of a *kura* (storehouse), it's common to find a white plaster surface with dark-framed windows scattered here and there. The long expanse of *kura* walls at the back of Higashi-Honganji on Horikawa street features a dramatic row of such windows.

When adjoining *kura* have been built at different times, the windows don't line up nicely as do those of Higashi-Honganji. On one wall, there will be three windows up high, and on the adjoining wall, maybe two down low. The spatial placement of the windows creates a "Mondrianesque" effect. My favorite of the "kura-wall" type is a city block of windows behind Bukkoji temple. It's a concert of black windows arranged in varying patterns in white plaster. When I take my friends on my "wall tour," we always go to see the back wall of Bukkoji. We never go inside.

———————

The Rule of Lightness

From plaster, we move on to hedges and fences. One could say that there's a sliding scale of walls, from "substantial" (the battlements of Nijo Castle), to "basic" (the lanes of Myoshinji), to "insubstantial" (garden fences). Over time, the emphasis shifted from heavier to lighter. Inside tea gardens or noble estates, rather than construct walls of brick or stone as the Chinese would have done, the Japanese built barriers made of bamboo, twigs, and branches—that is, fences instead of solid walls. Most common are the bamboo-type fences, which are tied together with dark twine made from palm fiber.

Emphasis on the insubstantial, the light touch, is another aspect of limination. While it's important to draw lines and make barriers, these don't need to be strong physical objects. A gate without a wall is as good as a gate with one. A fence made of twigs is as good as a wall of brick and mortar. All you need is the hint of a wall.

We could qualify limination and add the "rule of lightness." There's a paradox here, which must have deep roots in human psychology, which is: the lighter and more transparent the barrier, the more seriously we take it.

Court lady Sei Shonagon, author of the 11th century Heian classic *Pillow Book*, was a great list maker. She had a list of "Cute Things." One of them was "a child's face drawn on a melon." That's the very definition of *kawaii*. So we know that the *kawaii* concept dates back at least to Heian. As for limination and the rule of lightness, Sei Shonagon had another list of "Things Which Are Near Yet Far." It included "a picnic just outside the walls of the palace." The picnic might be near the palace, but it's *outside the wall*. So it's really, really far.

Limination is in our minds—it doesn't take much to draw those lines. So you can go light. And Japan, richly experienced with limination, is good at this. It's all about mood and attitude rather than physical barriers per se. With the rule of lightness in mind, it was perhaps inevitable that walls would tend towards lighter and more evanescent materials, ultimately arriving at fences and hedges.

Katsura Detached Palace should really be celebrated as much for its fences and hedges as for its buildings.

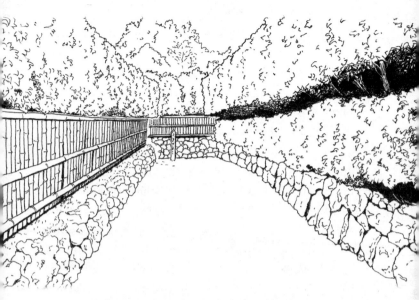

Ginkakuji-gaki fence of two levels (stone and bamboo),
topped by a camellia hedge

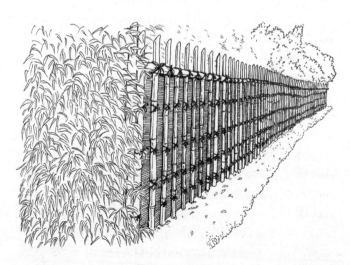

Hedge made from living bamboo merges into a rush-and-bamboo fence,
Katsura Detached Palace

You have parallel hedges that aren't quite parallel, giving you an illusion of perspective. You see a play of materials: thick and thin bamboo, lined up in vertical rows, or split and woven; bundles of rushes; and pruned hedges. There's even a type of hedge made from weaving together the branches of living bamboo. These hedges and fences lead you in a certain direction, hiding one view while drawing your attention to another.

Outside of Katsura, Kyoto's premier example of a hedge-wall would be the alley of greenery at the entryway to Ginkakuji. As you approach the temple grounds, you angle sharply to the right and then enter a narrow lane lined with tall camellia hedges. It's a composite fence of three levels: a stone wall at the bottom, a low bamboo fence on top of the stones, and rising from behind that, a tall hedge.

The two lower levels—stone topped by a bamboo fence—is a special combination known as *Ginkakuji-gaki* (Ginkakuji fence); while the central bamboo part alone has yet another name, *Kenninji-gaki* (Kenninji fence), for it was supposedly at Kenninji temple that they first started making fences like this. Fences, as we might have expected, have names—about 150 varieties—depending on what they're made of and the way they're bound together. There's *Daitokuji-gaki*, *Koetsuji-gaki*, *Ryoanji-gaki*, and many others, and these are just the names of fences used in temples.

Ginkakuji (Silver Pavilion) is something of a quandary. Much of what we now see was added in the centuries after the temple was first built. So who knows if those hedges are original? If so, I imagine that the sharp zigzag served the same purpose as the sudden tacking of the entry path at Nijo Castle—to make it hard for invaders to march right in. After all, Ginkakuji was built by a military shogun at a time of war.

Whether original, or added later, the hedge is incredibly successful. The hedgerows cut off the view, funneling visitors into a small channel. It makes you feel you've come to a secret and intimate place. It prepares you for a heightened "experience."

The prevailing view of Ginkakuji is that it epitomizes the rarified aesthetic of mid-Muromachi in the 15th century. Much ink has been spilled on the contrast between its restrained lack of silver, versus the lavish use of gold at Kinkakuji (Golden Pavilion); on how it's best viewed in moonlight because of its wide expanse of raked sand centered on a conical light-reflecting mound. However, in fact, the complex is a hodge-podge of things added at different times. It was never called "silver" until early Edo—so there's no reason to contrast it with Kinkakuji. And the raked sand and the mound were also added in early Edo, a century and a half after the shogun first built it.

Except for two buildings that remain from the original, it's not particularly representative of Muromachi. The high sand mound (which kept getting higher as the Edo period progressed) is typical of the over-the-top decorative impulse of Kabuki and woodblock prints. One suspects that the temple "did up" the garden to please 17th century tourists. The Muromachi mystique is a case of the "Emperor's New Clothes." And yet everyone who

visits Ginkakuji comes away deeply impressed. I think it's
because the fence sets them up for it.

―――――

Framed Views
People tend to call Japanese gardens "rock," "sand,"
or "moss" gardens. While they will always have rocks,
they might be a bit short on sand or moss. But they
will invariably have a fence or a wall. They should really
be called "wall and fence gardens." This brings us to
another aspect of the walls and fences, which is that they
function as frames.

One of my mentors, writer Donald Richie, used to
say, "Japanese art is not representational, it's presenta-
tional." What he meant was that the art doesn't aim to
be or to show the real thing; it presents an idealized
form. Think of flower arrangements. The Western-style
flower arrangement is placed in the middle of a table; you
walk around it and view it from any angle. The Japanese
arrangement has a *men* or "face." In order for the lines
of branches, leaves, and flowers to show at best effect,
they must be seen from one direction. The arrangement
perches in a particular spot—a *tokonoma*, an altar, or
other formal space—from which it is to be admired at a
precise angle and height. Likewise with gardens.

The classic Zen gardens are not to be confused with
nature. They're a painting of nature, which means that
they have to be framed, just as paintings in Japan or
China are mounted as scrolls or as screens. As with a
painting, you separate the work of art from everything

else, put an edging around it and "present" it for our enjoyment. The framing of a garden is its wall or fence. This makes the boundary as important to the design as the garden itself. At Ryoanji the crumbling, oil-stained old mud wall behind the Zen garden is itself designated a National Treasure.

We see a wall that acts as a frame while taking the form of a living hedge at Entsuji. In the middle of the hedge rise tall tree trunks of cryptomeria cedar, framing the distant view of Mount Hiei as perfectly as though it hung on your wall.

In Kyoto, one frame is sometimes not enough. A fence sets off the garden, and a wall encloses the temple. A larger wall may surround the whole *garan* complex, which symbolizes sacred Mount Sumeru and the mountains around it. Piercing the gates and walls, like the axis of the universe itself, runs the *sando* walkway, passing through gate after gate, leading us upward towards the sacred mountain.

The outer walls are supposed to mark the border between the sacred inside and the profane outside. Actually, in old Japan there wasn't much difference. It was all beautiful, inside and out. Today, however, the walls have taken on a new meaning. They separate the placid moss and weathered timbers of the old temples, "the dream of old Kyoto," from the dreary reality of blocky concrete apartment buildings, flashing signage, and parking lots just outside the gate. The role of the Cosmic Wall, protecting against the sea of chaos outside, is no longer merely symbolic. It's for real.

Characters for *Shin Gyo So*
written from left to right in
shin gyo so styles of calligraphy,
by Alex Kerr

Chapter 3

Shin Gyo So

真行草

Inspired by calligraphy, Japan developed a three-layered world view which still impacts contemporary arts today.

I f you compare Japan to China, one of the huge differences is that China is highly intellectual and Japan is not. China boasts millennia of philosophers and keeps on producing, if not philosophy, political propaganda, which is about thought or the control of thought. While Japan absorbed Chinese philosophy, it was more concerned with aesthetics—that is to say, how things feel rather than what they mean. If you were to list the great thinkers of China, you'd start with towering philosophers like Zhuangzi, Confucius, and Mencius, and end up (maybe) with Mao. But in Japan, you'd be quoting Zeami about Noh drama and Sen no Rikyu on Tea ceremony.

So people who love China versus those who love Japan tend to divide between the thinkers and the feelers; Japan gets the aesthetic types. That's unfortunate for Japan because those are the ones who tend to go all gooey and soft at the mere hiss of the steam coming out of a brazier in the tearoom. This is why so much of the literature on Japan is euphoric and expressional, lacking in analytical rigor.

That said, there's an anti-intuitive twist to this situation. Through their sense and feeling about the aesthetics of things, the Japanese have sometimes broken through to cosmic insights that the philosophers of China and other countries never did. There is a philosophy in Japan, but it's wordless.

No, in fact, there are plenty of words! And we hear a lot about them. There's *yugen* (mysterious beauty) associated with Noh drama; *ten chi jin* (Heaven, Earth, Man) underlying Ikebana; or *wa kei sei jaku* (Harmony, Respect, Purity, Tranquility), the theme of Tea ceremony. Nowadays terms like these have graduated to full-fledged official dogma, right up there with Chinese political slogans. Ask a tea master what he's doing, and his mouth will open, and you'll hear "*wa kei sei jaku*." But while these words sound nice, they don't mean much on their own. What's really the use of knowing that the tearoom should be "pure" or "tranquil"? It just doesn't tell you anything of value. The profundity of the insight lies behind the words, and is something that you could only appreciate when actually *doing* the Tea ceremony—that is, in an aesthetic context.

A Paradigm from Calligraphy

Of the many forms of Japanese aesthetic thought I believe that *shin gyo so* is one of the most thought-provoking, and it's had an indelible impact on the city of Kyoto. The concept comes from calligraphy. There are three basic ways to write kanji characters. One is "standard script," which is the official or "true" form that you see in a newspaper, a book, highway signs, and so forth. It consists of squarish letters with each stroke cleanly delineated. A clear-cut, stroke-by-stroke way of writing. This script had two names in Chinese: *kai*, the word normally used, and a variant term, *shin*, meaning "true."

Then there is *gyo*, which means "walking" or "running." In *gyo* the writing is a little more relaxed and you can cut a few corners and slide a few strokes into one another. Running script (sometimes called "semi-cursive") is still reasonably close to standard script, but feels freer. It's standard script written on the run.

The third form is *so*, which means "grass." This script, which in English we call cursive, is a kind of short-hand—flowing, abbreviated, and, unless you've studied it, rather difficult for modern people to read. Often the grass form can be completely unrecognizable. In fact the jots and squiggles of *so* look more like grass than anything else. The *so* style lends itself to really wild calligraphy because it's more freehand, and much faster to write, making it the favorite form of calligraphers.

These are the three types. All had long histories in China, and then came into Japan. So from a very early period the Japanese were familiar with standard (or "true"), running, and cursive: *shin gyo so*.

———————

Identity Crisis

Japan had a problem. It was that everything worthwhile came from China. Ceramics, paper, lacquer, temples, literature, poetry, kanji, baskets, furniture... Where do you want to begin? Chinese things were grand, elaborate, colorful, technically polished, refined, elegant, inventive... you name it. Here was Japan at the receiving end of this deluge of noble and fabulous Chinese things, and the question arose, "Well, who are we?"

And at some point, and I think it happened after the devastating Onin War of 1467–77, there was a breakthrough. This understanding came fairly late in Japanese history and it's not something that you would find in Heian or Kamakura.

When Japanese of the late 15th and 16th centuries looked at what was really innate to their country, they suffered an identity crisis. What they found was rough and primitive. Ise Grand Shrine, Japan's holiest religious site, is thatched; it's not tiled like a Chinese palace would be. They found palaces roofed with cedar chips, country houses with smoky fires burning in floor hearths. There was *Negoro* lacquer—thick, uneven, with splotchy black under layers showing through where the surface would wear away—hardly to be compared with Chinese lacquer, carved with exquisite detail as if it were jade or ivory. Their native pottery was ungainly, heavy, hand-molded from gritty brown clay, and mostly unglazed. If it was glazed, it might have been an accident in the kiln of ash falling and melting on it. Many pieces were misshapen, unbalanced; they had none of the technical control that you would find in a Song dynasty celadon, for example.

A Breakthrough Understanding

At this moment arose the idea that everything in the world, and in human relations, comes in three levels—formal, semi-formal, and informal. These were named *shin*, *gyo*, and *so*, as in calligraphy.

We have this in our lives in the West: formal as in black tie; semi-formal would be smart casual; informal is shorts or jeans and a T-shirt. Different people wear them at different times and in different situations. You don't mix them up. You wouldn't wear a T-shirt to a black tie dinner, just as you wouldn't show up at a beach party in a suit and tie.

Shin gyo so later penetrated deep into Tea ceremony. However, let's pause right here before we dive into the treacherous waters of Tea punctilio. Of all our chapters, this one is the most speculative. So tea experts, read no further! Some of what follows fits right in with the official systems of Tea schools; but not all of it does. There are unorthodox ideas here that an old tea master divulged to me, or I picked up from eccentric literati or art collectors. Other concepts arose from observing how traditional Kyoto people instinctively used and arranged things.

With that disclaimer off my chest, now let's get back to the tale of *shin gyo so* as it unfolded in late Muromachi. The tea masters took another look at these crude, clunky Japanese things, and declared them to be wonderful. I think that was the turning point when Japanese culture became what it is today.

This hierarchy is something that is very human; it is always there and transcends nearly any kind of a boundary. It's just that a) the history of kanji, and b) the pressure from China, led the Japanese to think in a new way. "There is in calligraphy true, running, and cursive script, and there is that country over there which consistently produces these exquisite things that are just beyond us; and here we are producing this rough unpolished stuff; and in between is Korea which is kind of civilized like China, but not quite… Huh… Three levels—China,

Korea, Japan." From there the concept of *shin gyo so* expanded to include a whole range of hierarchies.

There was manmade versus natural with something that's partly manmade in between. There was high, mid-level, and low; and close, middle-distance, and far. And this applied to other arts beyond calligraphy, in particular, painting.

Shin Gyo So in Ink

In Ming painting and later in Japan, there are three types of ink technique. One is where every little leaf and every rock and every wave in the ocean is painted clearly. This is *shin*-style painting. The Chinese came up with names for the strokes of painting everything—the shapes of twigs and branches, various types of rock surface whether round, pockmarked, jagged, fluted, or cut as with an ax. The painting itself may be simple, but if the tree has been painted so that you can see every leaf and every branch that would be the equivalent of a *shin* calligraphic character where you see every stroke.

Then there is a more relaxed version, which the flexible Chinese brush lent itself to. It is a looser way of painting: some impressionistic geese standing beside a few quick slashes of the brush that make up autumn reeds. That's *gyo*.

Finally there's an extremely cursive version called *haboku*, which means "splashed ink." Here you have a blot and that's a mountain, over there, a blip and that's a rock, and a bit of wash over there and that's the ocean.

Top: *Shin* painting   Bottom: *Gyo* painting

So painting (*haboku* style)

And just like that, it's a landscape. These different styles were seen as *shin gyo so.*

Another way to look at these three types of ink technique is "realistic, impressionistic, and abstract." Abstract is in a sense the cursive or shorthand version of something.

Sometimes it's enough to have just two of the three levels. Shinju-an subtemple at Daitokuji mostly dispenses with *shin*, concentrating on *gyo* and *so*. The main Zen hall features *gyo*-style paintings of birds and grasses painted in freehand by the enigmatic 15th century artist Soga Jasoku. Behind that is one of my favorite ink paintings in the city, a paper-covered wall (basically an unmovable *fusuma*) which is pure *haboku*—splashes and washes of ink that create a misty landscape, with a few birds, a rising sun with a slight bit of color, and that's it.

Credited to one of the painters in the Jasoku lineage, this painting is extremely abstract, one of the most abstract wall paintings in Kyoto. But in addition to its super-*so* style, its location within the temple is also significant. At Shinju-an, *gyo* is reserved for the main hall, and *so* is placed in the room behind it. Both the paintings and their placement are leveled.

———

The Power of Three

The tea masters began to play with the idea of *shin gyo so* in the late 16th and early 17th century. For example, a bronze container would be *shin* because it refers back to classical Chinese bronzes. Bronze would be placed in

Top: Bronze (China)   Right: Porcelain (Korea)   Left: Bamboo (Japan)

the middle of the *tokonoma* because the center is *shin*, and a little bit off center is *gyo* and *so*. In contrast with bronze as *shin*, ceramics would be *gyo* and bamboo or baskets would be *so*.

When Tea ceremony first came to Japan it was very much Chinese-oriented. The original Tea was quite lavish with the daimyo collecting fine celadon from China. Tea was about palatial venues attended by nobles who drank from imported Chinese ceramics. The big turning point in Tea came with the concept of *wabi*, which dates back to Murata Juko (1422–1502), a Zen monk at Daitokuji who was active in that crucial seventy-year period after the Onin War. Juko and his followers (the third-generation adherent was Sen no Rikyu, who established Tea as we now know it) came up with the idea that "we're going to go for *wabi* or rustic, countrified Tea, and get away from richness, bright color, and elegance."

So Juko, at Shinju-an, built what is thought to be the first tea garden. It's very simple—just three stones, five stones, and seven stones in a tiny plot no bigger than about a few tatami. By the time this idea reached Sen no Rikyu in the late 1500s, he was very aware that Japanese Tea was *wabi*. *Wabi* is *so*, in contrast to the *shin* of the original Tea, performed in palaces with flawless Song and Ming ceramics.

Rikyu went to Chojiro (?–1589), a maker of roof tiles, the humblest ceramic material you can think of, and asked the tile maker to create a tea bowl for him. That became *raku* ware, which instead of being high-fired and polished porcelain is low-fired earthenware.

In this way *shin gyo so* expanded from painting into ceramics. *Shin* would be fine porcelain, *gyo* stoneware, and *so* earthenware. And among earthenware, tile ware—which had hardly any other use except as roof tiles or flooring—was the lowest of them all. But Rikyu made *raku* the standard. People use all kinds of bowls today, but *raku* ware reigns supreme in Tea ceremony.

By the way, with the three types of ceramics, how do you know which one you're dealing with? Strike a porcelain bowl, and it gives out a resonant "ting"; do that with a stoneware ceramic and it goes "clink." But tap a *raku* earthenware piece, and it just goes "clunk." Ting, clink, and clunk are the *shin gyo so* of ceramic sounds.

From ceramics, on to architecture. A Chinese-style structure with glazed tiles, bracketed gables, and wide columns would be *shin*. A cedar-chip-roofed shrine would be *gyo*. A thatched farmhouse would be *so*. Instead of serious structures with great timbers and sweeping roofs, tearooms tended to be flimsy shacks, thatched or perhaps roofed with a light layer of *sugi* bark. The rooms are tiny, and the concept was that they were a compressed version of a farmhouse. That's why they brought the *irori* floor hearth into the tearoom, making it smaller and a little bit deeper so that it wouldn't dirty the tatami. It was like sitting by the hearth in your own mini-farmhouse, all of which is *so*.

This becomes more and more complex. They broke it down even further so that you can have *shin-no-shin*, that is, "*shin* within *shin*," or "ultra-formal." For example, if you displayed a Chinese bronze in the grand, gold-leafed painted *tokonoma* of a palace, that would be *shin-no-shin*. But if you held a Tea ceremony in that same room using ceramics instead of bronze, it would be *shin-no-gyo*, "*gyo* within *shin*." It would still be *shin* because you are in a palace, but you would have come down a step within *shin*. And you can have *so-no-so*, and *gyo-no-shin*, and on and on.

All of this has to do with the power of three. Three is a magical number in every country. Think of the Christian Trinity or the three orders of Greek columns (Doric, Ionic, and Corinthian), which look suspiciously like *shin gyo so*. But the Japanese developed a whole series of these triple states.

Another *shin gyo so* trio is colors: gold is *shin*; drab, earthy colors would be *so*; and bright colors in between would be *gyo*. When you walked into a gold-leafed environment in pre-18th century Japan, that would be *shin*; an earthy, monochrome space would be *so*; and people designed spaces with these concepts in mind.

———

Daisen-in Garden

There are many places in Kyoto where you can see the *shin gyo so* mechanism at work, but one of the most sophisticated examples would be the garden of Daisen-in subtemple in Daitokuji. It consists of three parts surrounding the main hall.

You start at the upper-right corner, at the top of the verandah on the right-hand side of the temple. You find there a meticulously designed version of a Chinese landscape painting, done in rocks, shrubbery, and sand. There are a few tall standing stones that are peaks, and here and there bits of pruned bushes that look like the mists commonly seen in landscape paintings. Between the stones, a bit of sand trickles down which represents a river flowing out of the mountain valley. From there the flow widens out to become a stream of sand running beside the verandah.

Now you're looking at a river of sand, and in the middle of it is a large boat-shaped rock. By the way, it's not a Japanese boat. It's a "treasure boat," shaped like one of the ships that used to trade with Ming China. This reminds us that we're still in the realm of a Chinese landscape painting.

Your perspective on the river of sand has moved much closer. At first you were gazing as though from a great distance at a misty mountain landscape. Now you're looking down on a river in which you can clearly see a boat. The stream and boat both suggest traveling, giving you now the sense that you're on a journey.

The verandah turns onto the wide patio fronting the temple, and as you round the corner, you behold a wide empty courtyard. It's the ultimate abstract Zen garden because it consists only of sand, with two mounds each about twenty centimeters high. You could interpret them as islands. Or they could be waves. Although it's customary to talk about "Zen rock gardens," this one has no rocks at all.

The three stages are *shin gyo so*. You started with a rock landscape done in fine detail; you went from there to the

Daisen-in garden (first part)

Daisen-in garden (second part)

Daisen-in garden (third part)

less detailed middle area consisting of a sand river with a boat-shaped rock; and then to very little detail—two mounds of sand rising out of raked gravel. It's a progression from pictorial, to impressionist, to abstract. The space went from compact, to medium, to wide.

You've gone from China and *shin*—a vertical landscape where the Daoist immortals dwell—to the flat white sand of Shinto shamans, which is Japan and *so*. The journey started with the material and ended in the immaterial. Your perspective went from far away, to medium, to very close.

Daisen-in garden is a book of three chapters, and in each one the plot takes a new twist: from the mountains of the immortals, down the river, to the wide sea. Compression and expansion of space. It's all presented through the metaphor of *shin gyo so*.

———————

The Power of *Gyo*

When you start looking for *shin gyo so*, you will find it in your own life, you will find it everywhere. But only the Japanese developed it to this level of finesse, and the best examples survive in Kyoto.

The whole thing began because of this problem of how does Japan fit in with China. In thinking about this, the tea masters took into account not only cultural differences, but their positions on the map: China, a continent to the west, and Japan, a group of islands to the east. So the geography of Japan's near neighborhood came into play. If China was going to be *shin* in the hierarchy, and

Japan was *so*, then it was natural to look across the sea to the country in the middle, Korea, and to see Korea as *gyo*. And indeed, much Korean art does feel like it falls neatly between Chinese and Japanese. Korean ceramics and tea bowls are so valued because they are the ideal *gyo*.

Korean things are more symmetrically and perfectly formed than Japanese, but they are not as polished and refined as the Chinese would be. They have this magical *gyo* quality, which is the appeal of Korea. Tea connoisseurs picked up on that quite early.

With Korea, or *gyo* in general, we're dealing with the "Goldilocks Principle." When applied to porridge, *shin gyo so* comes out as "too hot, just right, too cold." In other words, *gyo* is "just right." In calligraphy, running script (*gyo*) is looser than standard (*shin*), but not as difficult and unreadable as cursive (*so*). It falls in the middle, so it's the one most people actually end up writing.

In tea bowls too, *gyo* is "just right." In fact, when the Muromachi tea masters were creating *wabi*-style Tea, their first efforts were focused on Korean ceramics. They started using *ido-chawan*, rice bowls from the Korean countryside, which they appreciated as being "rough" and "artless." The tea masters adopted them and they've been National Treasures ever since. Only later did Rikyu and the others move on to appreciate the really rough Japanese *so* styles.

As a sideline, I wonder if Korean *gyo* isn't still strong today. Not as stylish or advanced as Apple's iPhone, but ahead of old-fashioned rivals like Nokia and Sony, "moderately advanced" Samsung conquered the smartphone market. Not as visceral as US rock music, but more lively than bland Japanese pop, "middle-of-the-road" Korean pop swept Asia. *Gyo* power lives on.

The Reversal of Taste

There is a final twist to this story, which is an unexpected one, but in a way is predetermined. *Shin gyo so*, as originally formulated, saw China as "high," Korea as "medium," and Japan as "low." But in the end, the whole thing gets stood on its head. The cultivated elite of Japan said, "*So* is better than *shin*."

It was because of national pride. A clunky, malformed bit of clay is to be more highly valued than anything so polished and manmade. Pale, drab, *shibui* colors are to be seen as attaining a higher, more sophisticated appeal than bright colors. The concept of imperfection—something broken, something worn—very *so* and not *shin*—came to be revered as the highest aesthetic. People who considered themselves well educated were taught, and eventually developed, the taste of *shibui*, preferring dull, rough, imperfect things to elaborately decorated, colorful, and well-finished things.

But let's not get carried away and try to define Japan just by *so*. Japan hankered after *shin* as much as anybody else—in fact it's my theory that frustrated attempts to match Chinese *shin* were what started the whole process in the first place. Gold is the ultimate *shin* color, and so in love with gold was Japan that they covered the Golden Pavilion at Kinkakuji—an entire temple—with it, something that to my knowledge the Chinese never did. They smeared gold over vast expanses of sliding doors and folding screens, creating a shining world very far from *so*. Not to mention the gorgeous costumes of Noh drama, the colorful glazes of Imari and Kutani ceramics, and so on.

Over the centuries Japan seems to go through phases, bouncing between the two poles of *shin* and *so*. In mid-Muromachi the shoguns and warlords favored *shin* as exemplified by the Golden Pavilion (1398); by the 1580s, Rikyu and the tea masters had made the shift to *so* with their shadowy tearooms and drab tea bowls. In the early 1600s, it was back to *shin* with the Edo Shogunate's massive building projects that produced the gold-leafed palaces of Edo and many of the grander temples of Kyoto that we see today.

Nowadays it's common for Westerners to see Japanese art as the pinnacle of minimalism and reserve. But a century ago, this was the last thing in people's minds when they thought of Japan. The art of Japan that first reached Europe and America in the 19th century was defined by painstaking detail and a riot of color: think woodblock *ukiyoe* prints, super-detailed Satsuma ware, gold screens, lavish kimono, and gorgeous painted fans. These things, plus geisha in their erotic finery, defined Japan's culture internationally. It took the West over a century to start appreciating Japan's "*so*" side. In fact, it took Japan about the same time to rediscover its *so* side.

So it's not that *so* conquered all. Far from it. Ikebana master Kawase Toshiro says, "Every country in the world had *shin gyo so*. Where the Japanese are different is that we're the only ones who made *so* into *shin*."

Eventually the imperfect, lumpy things got incredibly polished and refined by the tea masters. The levels reversed. What kind of *so* or *wabi* is a teahouse that costs a million dollars to build with specially chosen woods, or a rough tea bowl that can only be properly made by the descendant of an exalted lineage? *So* was turned into another type of *shin*. *Shin* in *so* clothing.

———————

The Beauty of Blah

As it happens, the two leading potters of Kyoto today, maybe the two leading potters of Japan—well, let's say the two leading potters of the world—have each staked out a position at an extreme pole of *shin* or *so*. Fukami Sueharu creates sleek forms with mathematically curved surfaces and knife-thin edges, made with total precision. He uses the purest white porcelain, overlaid with immaculate pale celadon glaze. These are *shin* objects, "art works" to be displayed in a museum.

Raku Kichizaemon XV, heir to the Raku tradition, produces rough, sandy-surfaced, splash-glazed tea bowls, with crudely chopped edges and uneven rims. You could put these in a museum—in fact, you can see *raku* bowls from fifteen generations displayed at the family's Raku Museum in downtown Kyoto, and there's a whole hall devoted to Kichizaemon's works at Sagawa Art Museum, located an hour out of town. But tea bowls don't work well in museums in the same way that Fukami's

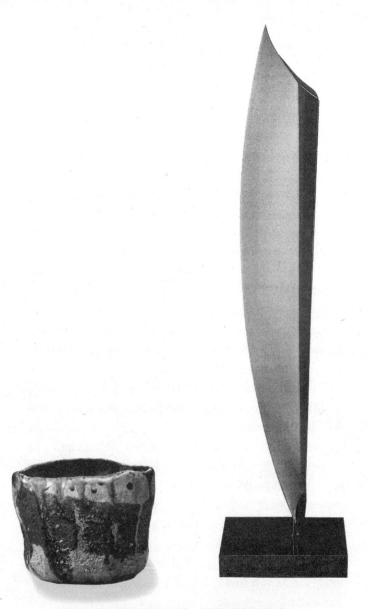

Right: Celadon sculpture "View II," by Fukami Sueharu
Left: Tea bowl "There is Shimmering Water on the Cliff III,"
by Raku Kichizaemon XV

sculpturesque ceramic art objects do. *Raku* bowls are just bowls after all, utilitarian objects to be brought out in a Tea ceremony and then put away. They're the ultimate *so*.

Which brings us to another *shin gyo so* trio of qualities: "fascinating, interesting, blah." Proust was impressed by a duchess who would pen three adjectives of praise in her letters—but in descending order. She would say, "I was overjoyed, delighted, pleased to meet your fabulous, charming, nice friends." The scale of adjectives goes the wrong way. "Pleased" and "nice" are ordinary and therefore seem more of a put-down than praise. We look down on the ordinary. In art, we positively fear it. "Blah" is something we all try to avoid. Yet the Japanese, supremely of all people on earth, discovered the glory of blah, and called it good. It was part of the same revolution that brought in the appreciation of *so*.

When it came to gardens, the Chinese strewed the grounds with towering rocks, each more twisting and filled with intriguing ins-and-outs than the next. These "spirit stones" writhe and flicker like rising smoke or wind-blown mists, and in their grotesquerie the Chinese saw the movement of the Dao. The Japanese, however, chose rocks of no particular distinction, this one a little pointier than the next perhaps, but mostly looking like perfectly ordinary boulders. Blah, that is. They half-buried these in the earth, making them look even more blah. And from this sprang the beauty of Japanese gardens loved worldwide.

The same thing happened with tea bowls. The usual way to look at *raku* bowls is to see them as "rough"

Top: Chinese rocks in Yuyuan garden, Shanghai
Bottom: Japanese rocks at Entsuji temple

or "naturalistic." The truer way might be to call them "blah." The shape of a tea bowl is basic and doesn't vary much; the glazes are dull and not especially arresting. This goes back to a Zen idea, *heijoshin*, "the spirit of ordinariness." Zen tells us that our minds should be steady, not swayed by beauty or ugliness, sadness or happiness, excitement or boredom. All material things are illusion, so whatever shape a tea bowl takes, it's all the same. A blah tea bowl is as good as any other.

Having said that, the trick is how to make the ordinary extraordinary, blah into bling. Here's where the challenge arises. Anyone can appreciate the fascinating. Who can find beauty in the ordinary? That's Japan's extreme achievement.

The Best of Friends

Returning to potters Raku and Fukami, Fukami's shapes are exquisite and fascinating, that is, *shin*. Raku's bowls are mere baked clods of earth. Yet they rivet the attention. That is *so*. Each of these artists claims that the other one is the only potter who can truly understand him. This suggests one key to the secret of Japanese arts, which is that *shin* and *so* always co-exist, hiding within each other.

Sawada-sensei, under whom I studied Tea, told me that when he was a young man, he was invited to a ceremony hosted by Madame Deguchi Naohi, "The Third Spiritual Leader of Oomoto." David Kidd used to call her the "Mother Goddess." In her august presence,

Sawada tried to be on his best behavior, sitting at rigid attention, knuckles on the floor, back straight. Very *shin*. Naohi scolded him, "What's this over-formality? Can't you be a little more human in the tearoom?" The next time Sawada was invited, he sat at ease, hands in his lap, shoulders relaxed. Very *so*. Naohi snapped, "Where do you think you are? How can you be so slovenly and impolite?" It went on that way for years; he could never get it right. Then one day he noticed that he'd been sitting in the tearoom for hours but Naohi hadn't said anything. He realized that at some point he'd absorbed formality into informality, and no matter how he sat, it was all the same. *Shin* and *so* had merged.

Shin gyo so has so many ramifications that one could call it a cosmic idea. Concepts like this lend Japanese art a philosophical depth that's hard to find elsewhere. This is how people get addicted to Japan. They feel that the shape of a tea bowl is connected to great secrets of the universe. So aesthetic perception may be more powerful than we think. Maybe there *is* something ineffably important about the hiss of tea boiling in a tearoom.

Just in Time

By the time the Muromachi wars came to an end and Kyoto was rebuilt in the early 1600s, *shin gyo so*, and the reversal of taste whereby *so* was exalted over *shin*, came to influence the whole city: gardens of moss, simple small tearooms, the ethos of unpainted wood and *shibui* colors, all of those things played a role in why Kyoto looks the way it does and why people are drawn to Kyoto. For here is where it departs from China, where every surface gleams with cinnabar, every roof beam is painted. A noble bronze from which sprouts a stem of splendid peony blossoms stands symmetrically placed atop an elegantly formed table.

In Japan what do you find? A flimsy little tearoom with a woven-bamboo ceiling and some bare tatami, with a basket in the *tokonoma* that's not even centered, containing a few wildflowers and long grasses.

Another aspect of *shin gyo so* has to do with your view of life. *Shin* is about being proper, sitting straight, stiff upper lip. *Gyo* is day-to-day normality. *So* is about being outlandish, sexy, comic. Arranging this in a *shin gyo so* hierarchy, you get "serious, normal, funny."

In line with Japan's natural leaning towards *so*, early on came a trend towards the comic in art. You can see it in the hand scroll *Choju Jinbutsu Giga*, "Frolicking Animals" (ca. 1200), preserved at Kozanji in western Kyoto, in which rabbits and frogs cavort like human beings (copies of which feature on many a tourist trinket sold in Arashiyama today), or another Kamakura scroll, *Hohi Gassen*, "The Farting Contest." These scrolls are so cute and playful that one tends to simply enjoy them for their humorous charm without realizing how rare they are. In fact they're relics almost without peer in Asia.

I don't know of any important funny scrolls in either China or Korea. While comedy obviously must have existed

Hohi Gassen, "Contest of Breaking Winds" (detail)
Suntory Museum of Art

everywhere, only in Japan would silly things like these be preserved. Elsewhere, comedy was just too low to be valued. In its love of little ironic doodles, Japan was following the advice I once was given by David Kidd. "There's nothing worse than being serious," he scolded me. "But if you have to be serious, be serious about small things."

When you get into the Edo period, there was a further development in the comic area of painting, namely the cartoon-like images often used with haiku. They are called *haiga*, "paintings to go with haiku," and Zen monks like Sengai penned thousands of them. There's a manga-esque playful quality about *haiga*.

The Chinese literati turned in the other direction. There was a brief period in early Qing, when the Ming loyalist Bada Shanren did drawings with a lot of personality emerging from a few strokes of the brush. Bada Shanren's playful crows seem to be giving us a knowing smirk. But that was exceptional. The mainstream after that reverted to formality: rocks and mountains with the appropriate calligraphic inscriptions. Ever so proper. And the emphasis was usually on detail—often interesting and quirky detail—but still it focused on the fineness of the work. In ceramics, craftsmen vied to create more complex shapes with sophisticated and difficult-to-produce glazes. These gorgeous tours-de-force are the pieces that sell for tremendous prices in Chinese auctions today.

Whereas in Japan, things went increasingly in the direction of lumpy, misshapen, fire-burned bits and pieces, or humorous drawings that looked more like cartoons. Comedy in China was never much appreciated, at least among the educated elite, but scrolls by the Japanese literati leaned to the funny and sketchy. So Japan and China really diverged.

Today, with Ando Tadao and Taniguchi Yoshio's spartan architecture, Miyake Issey's wrinkled and pleated fashion, stark black-and-white photographs of sea horizons by Sugimoto Hiroshi, manga-esque playful drawings by Murakami Takashi, and the work of Raku and other potters making rough pieces out of stoneware and earthenware, *so* is having a resurgence in Japan.

And it came along just in time, as China came roaring back onto the world stage and is set to sweep all before it. But despite China's new strength, Japan keeps a commanding lead in the world when it comes to design. It will take at least a generation, maybe a century, for the Chinese to figure out how to compete with Japanese minimalism. *So* is doing all over again what the Muromachi tea masters set out to do in the 16th century: give Japan an identity.

The traditional Japanese perspective was that since China is *shin*, Japan must be *so*, and indeed, those were the directions that they followed. I think it also has to do with personality. What country are you going to fall in love with? If you're a *shin*-type person and like balance, refinement, elegance, polish, and reasoned philosophical thought, you are going to go for classical Chinese culture. But if you like the primitive, abstract, sensuous, and comedic—and don't mind blah—you'll go for Japan. And if you like something in between, there's always Korea. So, you can actually ask yourself: am I *shin*, *gyo*, or *so*?

Floor at Jisso-in, *Taki-no-ma*
(Waterfall Room)

Chapter 4

Floors

床

Look carefully at the floor.
Because you are where you walk.

There is a Zen adage that says something like "Watch your step." It's *Kan-kyakka!* (看脚下), literally "Look at what's under your feet!" This being Zen, it needs to be written as a shout, with an exclamation point. The moment matters! Each footstep that you take is important! It's also about being grounded: Don't keep your eyes in the clouds. Look down at where your feet are walking.

So, in this chapter, that's what we'll do. We'll look at floors.

The world knows Japan as the land of tatami mats, and it mostly still is today. But Japan didn't begin as tatami. I learned that early on in the 1970s when I bought an old farmhouse in the mountains of Shikoku. That house, named Chiiori, was three hundred years old with two *irori* (floor hearths), square sunken pits cut into the middle of the rooms, in which a fire was always burning. Around the *irori*, spread out wide were floors made of pinewood planks, blackened from smoke and shiny from centuries of people walking over them. Not a tatami to be seen.

Later, in Kyoto, I noticed that in certain old Zen temples there will be a broad wooden floor in the main hall, and around the edges are two rows of tatami, placed there as though an afterthought. And while these temples had a mix of tatami and wooden flooring, Shinto shrines only had wooden decks and stages. So there was a time before tatami.

Much later in the 1990s, when I started spending time in Southeast Asia, I found that the houses of Thailand and Southern China look remarkably like Chiiori. They're raised up on stilts; the flooring is wood planks; the roofs are thatched with leaves or grass; people take their shoes off before going inside. It seems obvious that Japanese house architecture came from Southeast Asia, not from Northern China.

This shows up in many ways. For example, the crossed beams rising from the thatched roof of Ise Grand Shrine are closely related to what you would see in Chiangmai, Thailand.

So are roofs that expand outwards at the top so that the upper ridge sticks out. The roofline starts out wide at the ridge, narrows in the middle, and then flares out again at the bottom. Using typeface, you could describe this shape like this: >—<. It's a typical shape for an old Japanese farmhouse. Fine examples of such roofs stand in the well-preserved village of Miyama-cho, northwest of Kyoto. Similar roofs are found in Indonesia and other places in Southeast Asia. These are the ancient indigenous roofs of Japan.

In contrast, Chinese roofs swoop downwards from the top ridge, with no narrowing. You could type that shape as: /‾\. After centuries of Chinese influence, both styles can be found in Japan today. Related to the Chinese roof would be the temples of Kyoto; whereas the primeval Japanese expanding roof can be seen in *minka* all over Japan. In Kyoto, you can find elegant thatched

Roofs with extending crossbeams
Top: Chiangmai, Thailand
Bottom: Ise Grand Shrine

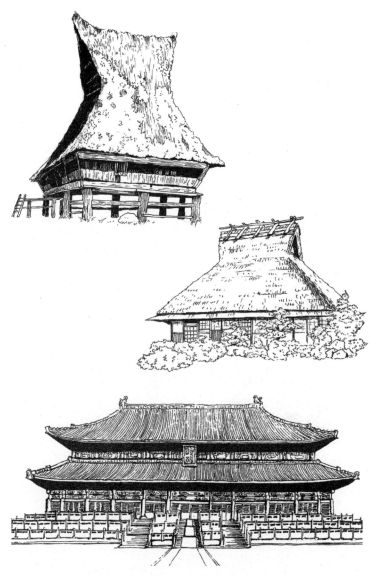

Roofs with expanded upper sections:
Top: Indonesia   Middle: Miyama-cho, Kyoto Prefecture
Bottom: Chinese-style roof sweeping downwards from narrow ridge,
Forbidden City, Beijing

farmhouses with such roofs in the Sagano area, especially around Daikakuji temple.

Another Southeast Asian trait found in Japan is the raising of buildings on stilts. In Southeast Asia the stilts are a full story high, and a relic of this can still be seen in Japan at the 8th century Shoso-in treasury in Nara, where the pillar-supports stand two-and-a-half meters high.

In Japan, certain shrines and palaces went on having extremely high verandahs. But gradually the stilts came down until the modern Japanese house is raised only thirty to eighty centimeters above the ground. People don't think of the supports under Japanese houses as "stilts" because they're low, but that's what they are.

On top of those stilts they laid wooden floors. Here is a big difference between the countries that took China as the keynote for daily living, and the others. China-oriented countries (China, Vietnam, Tibet, and Korea) use chairs, tables, stands, furniture, and the other countries do not. In Indonesia, Thailand, Laos, and Burma, you have empty, smooth wooden floors, and people take off their shoes because they sit on the floor. It's the same in Japan. You don't walk around inside with dirty, muddy shoes where you sit and eat and live. But in China, people customarily entered wearing their shoes because floors were earthen or tiled, and you never sat down on those floors. Instead they used chairs.

Building on stilts, Northern Thai house

Shoso-in treasury, Nara

Black Glistening

So the wooden floor is the starting point for Japan. In the old farmhouses, smoke from the *irori* would darken the floors, the columns, the pillars, and the underside of the thatch, turning the whole place into a black, shiny surface. It seems almost lacquered black. That *kuro-bikari*, so-called "black glistening," is what you can still see in ancient situations like Chiiori. And I imagine that every old interior in Japan would have looked like that.

In Kyoto you can still get a glimpse of this in certain places. If you're a connoisseur of *kuro-bikari*, then the supreme black floors are to be found at the Imperial Abbey of Jisso-in in the northeast. In their deep-black sheen, you can see reflected the garden beyond, green in the spring, orange and yellow in the fall, white in the winter. Ghostly images emerging from glossy black.

There's another black floor that deserves mention—on the third story of Kinkakuji (Golden Pavilion). Burned down by a crazy monk in 1950, the temple was rebuilt in 1955, so this floor is not old. The third story stands almost empty except for a small reliquary in the center, surrounded by an immaculate floor of black lacquer, polished like glass. In this shimmering black surface are perfectly reflected the gold-leafed walls and ceiling of the room—one of the more surreal sights of Kyoto. However, I know this only from photographs. The interior of Kinkakuji is never open to the public, so we just have to take satisfaction in knowing that this floor is there. I'm not sure if the original Muromachi

Black glistening floors at Chiiori

floor would have been like this. Maybe it's just an invention by an academic in the Cultural Ministry who did some study and thought the floor "ought" to look like this. Kyoto is full of faux re-creations like that. But whatever the case, the third-story floors of Kinkakuji are truly extraordinary.

A rare variation on this is when they lacquer the floors red. In the back of Daikakuji there's a pavilion called Reimeiden, which was built in 1928 in Tokyo and moved in 1958 to Daikakuji. It's a relatively young building for Kyoto. The floors are lacquered bright vermillion, and they're reflective, like the *kuro-bikari* floors of Jisso-in. Look down and you see the gilded hinges of the temple doors swimming in a pool of vermillion lacquer.

Advent of Tatami

But of course, Japan does have tatami. They developed from *mushiro*, crude mats made from rice straw, which they used to spread over the wooden floors of farmhouses. We used *mushiro* at Chiiori until recently because they're thick and soft and quite comfortable to sit on. But we stopped because *mushiro* shed constantly. We were always sweeping away bits and pieces of rice straw or brushing it off our clothes.

Historically, the solution to the *mushiro* shedding problem came with the advent of *igusa*, a kind of rush that is water-resistant and durable. *Igusa* could be woven tightly into a thin smooth mat, called a *goza*. *Goza* look nice, but they're too thin to give much relief to a backside in pain from sitting for a long time on a hard wooden floor. So, to sum up the history of tatami, they combined *mushiro* and *goza*, coming up with a stuffed mat, about two inches thick, of which the interior is made from soft rice straw like the old *mushiro*, and the surface is covered with sleek woven *goza*. That's what a tatami is, a *mushiro* and *goza* sandwich.

Along came the Chinese input, which was the concept of the *importance* of mats. In China, the use of floor mats went back for millennia, with mats only fading away after the Song dynasty (960–1279), when they switched once and for all to tables and chairs. In the 5th century BC *Confucian Analects*, it's written that "The Master would not sit down if his mat was not straight" (席不正不座), meaning that things should be done correctly, with everything in its proper place. The importance of the mat on which you sit survives in an expression like *zhuxi*, literally "main mat," which is the modern Chinese word for Chairman, as in "Chairman Mao."

Actually, it wasn't until Heian that they invented the stuffed tatami. Aristocrats and nobles took to sitting on a single tatami, much thicker and higher than the ones we have today, which differentiated them from lesser people who would have to sit on the wooden floor. Once you had raised mats, you had a brand new way to signify status. For a circle of rank-obsessed aristocrats, who until then had had to share the floor with their inferiors, it must have come as a godsend. Rules quickly proliferated. As early as the *Engishiki*, a 10th century book of ritual, there was already a regimen that defined the size and style of brocade edging allowed to nobles of different ranks.

Eventually by the Muromachi period, high-class places like temples and palaces began to cover the entire floor with these raised mats. In the process, they reduced the thickness to the four-centimeter size we have today. Another thing that happened around the same time is that architecture became modular, that is, all sizes were based on a standard measure. It was the distance between two columns, called a *ken*.

One square *ken* is the measure of an area called a *tsubo* (3.3 square meters). It's still used in modern real estate transactions to quantify land and house areas. Take that square-shaped *tsubo*, divide it in two, and you have space to lay two rectangular mats, each of them one *ken* long and half a *ken* wide. That's the birth of the modern standardized tatami. And because the houses were modular—they all used the same *ken* size—you could lay tatami in any room, anywhere, and they would fit.

By the Edo period, tatami had expanded out of palaces into domestic architecture, with normal homes also filling their rooms with these rectangular mats. They ended up with what we think of today as the typically tatami-matted space. But the tatami are actually resting on a wooden floor. If you pull them up, there is the wooden floor from Southeast Asia underneath.

It's typical of the way Japan takes in foreign influence. It doesn't wholly discard the old; it just adds the new on top. In their buildings, they kept stilts below, but replaced thatch with tile on top; they went on laying wooden floors, but spread tatami over them.

———————

Tatami and Status

Once tatami took over wooden floors, everything changed. Many a treatise has been written about how Japanese society evolved during Kamakura, Muromachi, early Edo, and so forth. But era names like Muromachi and Edo don't mean much. Just because the era had changed, and a new family ruled from the shogun's castle, why would people do anything differently? There should be a more accurate book entitled *The Transformation of Japan's Social Order after Tatami*.

To see what this involves, we need to go back to the original tatami, which was a stuffed mat raised higher than the rest of the room. It's where the noble sat. This meant that a room had a "high" part and a "low" part, and people sat in the part that their status entitled them to be in, or on.

That was easy when you had just one or two raised mats and the rest was wood. But after Muromachi, when they covered the entire floor with tatami, they still needed to differentiate between an Emperor and, say, second-tier aristocrats or samurai. So they began designing rooms of which one part would be raised. They called this area the *jodan-no-ma*, "upper-level room."

You can see it in structures around Kyoto that have an Imperial background (many were once part of a palace and later moved somewhere else), such as Shugaku-in

Three levels of floor at the Imperial Palace, Kyoto

Detached Palace, the Imperial Abbey of Shoren-in, Jisso-in, as well as the Imperial Nunnery of Reikanji. Once you start looking for them, you find that *jodan-no-ma* are quite a common feature of old Kyoto, surviving in dozens of temples and palaces. Wherever a royal backside once rested, the floor must forever be raised.

Even having a raised floor wasn't quite enough height for imperial dignity, so in the *jodan-no-ma*, they would place yet another tatami on top of the dais. This would be an *atsu-tatami* (thick tatami) about ten centimeters thick, an echo of the original thick mats that they sat on in Heian. These *atsu-tatami* impress us even today, because they imply not only rank, but harken back to ancient times, bringing into a room a whiff of Heian.

The Imperial Palace features a spacious tatami room called the Otsune-goten laid out in three floor levels, plus an *atsu-tatami* raising the Emperor to a fourth level. Each rise is only about ten centimeters, but succeeds in creating an ineffable sense of the distant imperial majesty.

At the main audience hall of Nijo Castle they installed two levels of floor. The higher level was of course where the shogun or his appointed governor held court; then there was a lower tier for descending ranks of noble pages, high lords, and finally, everyone else. They've got wax effigies in silk kimono laid out in the hall, so you can see just how it worked.

Kamiza and *Shimoza*

It's only in a regal kind of space that you get an actual rise in the level of the floor. Most floors are simply flat. Or at least they look flat to our eyes. But people had got accustomed to the idea that rooms have a "higher" and a "lower" end. As a rule, the area closest to the *tokonoma* is the *kamiza* (upper seat) and the area nearest the entrance, usually at the other end of the room, is the *shimoza* (lower seat). The room flows from higher to lower, with the guest of honor sitting in the *kamiza*. The other guests and the host align themselves on downwards, towards the *shimoza*.

Today the *kamiza-shimoza* rule holds true everywhere in modern Japan. In a restaurant the guest of honor will sit near the *tokonoma*, facing outwards with the *tokonoma* to his back. The person with the lowest status will sit at the end of the table closest to the exit.

This also applies to corporate reception rooms where the basic rule is that the window to the outside corresponds to the *tokonoma*. The main guest will usually sit by the window in the seat farthest from the entrance. The other blue suits arrange themselves in descending order at distances farther away from the window. The suits may look identical, but by where they are sitting, these people's status is as clear as if they wore badges around their necks reading "VIP" and "minion."

How to sit in the right place at a business meeting is the kind of thing that's taught to American businesspersons in those classes they take about Japanese etiquette.

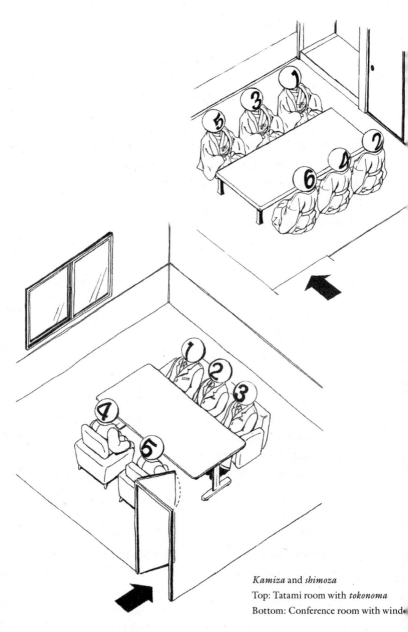

Kamiza and *shimoza*
Top: Tatami room with *tokonoma*
Bottom: Conference room with wind‹

140

They need to learn where to sit, how to hand a business card, and so forth, in order to cinch the deal. And they had better get it right, because *kamiza-shimoza* is a rigid, almost unbreakable rule. Put a group of Japanese in a room, and they will instinctively seek out the *kamiza* and arrange themselves accordingly. Companies try to get around this by building a room with no *tokonoma*, or an alcove that runs the full length of a wall; or they design a corporate meeting room with no windows. Even so, although temporarily baffled, people will figure out where the *kamiza* is.

While the visitor to Kyoto sees an expanse of tatami mats as a level surface, you'll need to tilt your head upwards or downwards to view the room at its proper perspective. Especially in the old days, people saw those rooms as having a marked slope. Depending on one's status, getting from the doorway to the *tokonoma* could be quite a climb. If the room belonged to a high noble, and even today, if you're in the inner chambers of one of the Tea ceremony headquarters, that *tokonoma* can feel as high as Mount Everest. The difference being, Everest is easy. Nowadays hundreds of people climb Mount Everest every year, but only a few ever gain access to those lofty *tokonoma*.

━━━━━━

Tatami Edgings

Unlike wood floors, where every plank looks like another, tatami have cloth edgings. Vary the cloth or brocade, and you have more ways to indicate status. A border can be purple, black, or green. Its pattern might be picked out in white, yellow, or gold threads. Or it might feature a crab-like pattern of black on white, called *korai-beri* (Korean edging), which ranks high and is used for priests and nobles. The thick *atsu-tatami* found in shrines and palaces will be trimmed with an extra-wide edging, reserved only for the most honored, known as *ungen*, or "striped brocade."

Set off one by one with cloth edgings, tatami create a visible grid. They function like the chalk markings on a stage that let the ballerina know where to place her feet. There's a room called Hosensai at the Urasenke Tea Headquarters in which two of the tatami are edged with *korai-beri* because the room was designed to receive a particular noble, and this marks the spot where he was to sit. We often hear the preachment about how "everyone is equal once they enter the tearoom," but just look at the tatami edging, and then think again about how equal they are.

There is a villa that I have long admired in the grounds of Kachu-an in Arashiyama. It had been the property of 1910s painter Takeuchi Seiho, but then went through various hands. Kachu-an was never open to the public, but at one point when the previous owner had gone bankrupt and it was lying vacant, I got friendly with the caretaker and managed to get in a few times. There was an old thatched teahouse, and adjoining it a fine Taisho-era mansion. The floors were made of

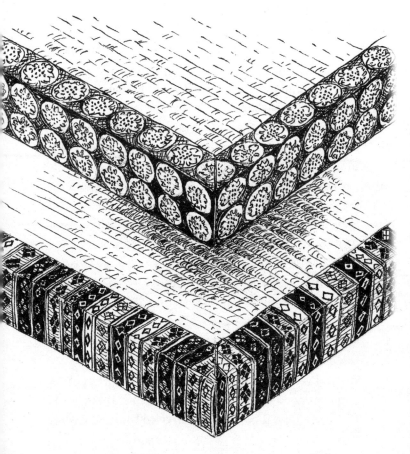

Top: *Korai-beri* "Korean edging"   Bottom: *Ungen* "striped brocade"

rare woods. The garden was enormous. I remember that along the corridor there were *fusuma* sliding doors that had been mounted with *ungen* edgings from *atsu-tatami* in the old royal palace. Being Imperial insignia and not the sort of thing that commoners could sit on, instead of putting them on the floor they were remounted on the doors.

The Japanese were masters at manipulating people through the psychological power exerted by simple things like *atsu-tatami* and *ungen*. In China, there was nothing subtle about imperial majesty. They exalted their Emperors on towering thrones, carved and embellished with gold lacquer and inlaid with jade. In Japan, just a few inches of raised tatami was enough to conjure the mystique. It elevated the Emperor as high as if he were floating on a cloud.

When you ponder Japanese history, it's close to miraculous that the Imperial family survived millennia of struggle and warfare without somebody trying to dethrone and replace them. They were often weak; it must have been tempting to the ruthless warlords who ruled the land. In bad times, the Emperors lost everything, lived in hovels. And yet those few inches of tatami continued to remind everyone of their untouchable divinity. Could it be that they survived because of where they sat?

━━━━━━━

Chinese Imperial Throne, Forbidden City, Beijing

Atsu-tatami mat at the *Hiru Goza* reception room, Imperial Palace

145

Outer corridor of Higashi-Honganji temple

About Wood

Let's set the subject of tatami aside for a moment, and get back to wood. Tatami appeared later as a temporary covering for wood, which was the more ancient and basic form of Japanese flooring. The wood never disappeared, and we find vestiges of it retained in parts of a Japanese house to this day, especially verandahs.

By the way, the verandahs of modern houses are usually half a *ken* wide, that is, just the width of one tatami. But in the old temples and palaces of Kyoto you see verandahs that are a full one *ken* deep, or at Nijo Castle, even more. Those broad expanses of polished wood, cool and shadowed, are among my favorite spaces in the city.

Having started out at wood-floored Chiiori, I'm a "wood appreciator," always on the lookout for fine grain, or that special sheen, and there's no better place to appreciate wood than the corridors of Kyoto. Curiously, while Japan is known as the "land of wood," with a rich tradition of all-wooden architecture, you don't hear very much about what type of wood this really was.

So I guess it's time for a little talk about wood. Along with the myth that "Japan's floors are always tatami," there's another one, which is "Japan's wood is always cedar." This arises from the fact that since the 1950s Japan's mountains have been stripped of their native forest cover and replanted with cedar. The cedar comes in two types, white *hinoki* and cheap industrial *sugi*. *Hinoki* was traditionally used in shrines, prized for its

148

clean whiteness; further, because it's water-resistant, it often features in outdoor corridors and decks. *Sugi*, despite its beautiful English name of cryptomeria, is a low-quality wood, soft, prone to cracks and knots, and useless for fine flooring or furniture. The government has promoted *sugi* plantations across Japan because *sugi* is fast-growing industrial timber useful for three-by-four beams in modern construction.

In my work of restoring old houses, when it comes to finishing the interiors, we need to come up with attractive materials for floors, walls, and furniture. Before *sugi* plantations took over the land, Japan once abounded in deciduous hardwoods like cherry, chestnut, and *keyaki* (Japanese elm). But today, one of the stranger paradoxes of modern Japan is that in this "land of wood," there's no wood to be had—that is, if you want to design a good modern chair, or put in beautiful flooring. There's just *sugi*. So in the end we've had to import oak, elm, and chestnut from North Carolina.

But having planted all that *sugi*, they must use it. There's quite a thrust from the authorities nowadays to build *sugi* structures, especially when public money is involved. When you see prized examples of modern Japanese wooden architecture, especially public buildings, it's almost universally done in *sugi*. An example would be JR Nijo station in Kyoto. The lower part is I-beams and the upper part consists of a geodesic framework of *sugi* timbers expanding into what could be described as an elongated Japanese umbrella. You also see coffee shops and some *machiya* redone in *sugi*, whose rough knotty texture gives them an American log cabin effect.

Actually, neither *hinoki* nor *sugi* are to be found much in old Kyoto, with the exception of Shinto shrines. Shinto prefers *hinoki* because it's white. Also, in ancient times, temples such as Horyuji utilized *hinoki*, but in general, for temples and houses, *hinoki* is too white, and has been avoided. Kyoto is brown and grainy, and not just because it aged. They built it that way. Rather than wait for time to do its work, homeowners used to coat pillars and beams with *kakishibu* (persimmon juice), so that the beams would darken even faster. Meanwhile, *sugi* may have plenty of grain, but it's too coarse, it will never take a polish, and old Kyoto is about nothing if it isn't about polish. So *sugi* was out.

————

Fine Woods

For most non-Shinto structures in the city they used *tsuga*. Known in English as "Southern Japanese hemlock," *tsuga* is a kind of pine. Typically they built temples and palaces using *tsuga* for pillars and beams, and *akamatsu* (red pine) for the floors, as at Chiiori. Red pine is a favorite for floors because it's rich in sap, and over centuries as the wood slowly exudes sap, the waxes and oils create a distinctive shine.

Noh drama stages, derived from shrines, are made with the favorite wood of Shinto, *hinoki*. A "neutral" wood, it has no particular color, grain, or luster. Just right for a performance space. With Noh stages they're inordinately careful about the floor, lest it get stained from the oils of mortal feet. Heaven help you if you forget for a moment and try to step onto a Noh stage in normal socks, or worse, barefoot. Panicked assistants will rush forward to prevent such a catastrophe. Only *tabi* (split-toed socks) will do for keeping a Noh stage clean and polished. (By the way, I'm reminded that David Kidd used to define *tabi* as "bifurcated foot mittens.")

From late Edo and into Meiji, they developed a taste for more luxurious woods. *Keyaki*, a type of elm, which had been used for fine *tansu* chests because of its deep orange-red color and strong grain, now came to be spread as flooring in the outer corridors and *tokonoma* of wealthy homes. It was beautiful and expensive, and so signified that you were rich. You sometimes find *keyaki* pillars in Kyoto's older temples, dating back to the days when Japan still had forests of magnificent towering *keyaki* trees, now all but extinct. You can see dramatic examples in the *keyaki* pillars of Myoshinji and Sennyuji temples' main halls.

The grandest *keyaki* construction of them all is the Goeido hall of Higashi-Honganji temple. Completed in 1895, its vast roof is supported by ninety massive *keyaki* pillars, which were donated by believers from all over the country. This was the last major building to be built with *keyaki* in Japanese history, and it will very likely never be possible again. Unless, of course, they start planting *keyaki* instead of *sugi*...

Moon-viewing platform at Katsura Detached Palace

You do see a lot of *keyaki* as an upscale accent in late 19th and early 20th century *machiya*, shops, and restaurants. And as Japan grew richer with the post-Meiji industrial revolution, wealthy homeowners and shopkeepers graduated from *keyaki* to even more expensive woods. By the Taisho period (1912–26), the homes of the elite featured rare woods such as *kuri* (chestnut) and Chinese hardwoods like *shitan* (purple sandalwood) and *karin* (red-orange quince). Those were the sorts of floors I had seen at Kachu-an.

━━━━━━

Moon Viewing

As a general rule, you could say that tatami are found where people live and sleep, and wood in the areas that they walk on or through. This is especially true of covered walkways in the garden that lead you from one building to another. These open-sided corridors get a lot of rain, so they need to be floored in a water-resistant wood, which is often *hinoki*. One of the most extensive networks of these walkways, connecting in zigzags from one hall to another, is to be found at Daikakuji. They not only zigzag laterally; they rise and fall in stepped cascades as you move from one pavilion to another. Meandering through moss and trees, these roofed passageways conjure up something of the courtly life of ancient times.

Open wooden decks facing a garden or pond are another thing that reminds us of Southeast Asian origins. You find them in Thailand, but never in China. One of

Kyoto's most famous wooden decks is the *tsukimi-dai* (moon-viewing platform) of Katsura Detached Palace.

David Kidd admired it so much that he had a replica built in his garden when he lived in Ashiya. On crisp November evenings we used to dress up in Tibetan robes, go out onto David's moon-viewing platform, and read Chinese poetry while sipping tea and gazing at the moon.

On a less decadent note, there's the broad deck of Kiyomizu temple, perhaps Kyoto's single most visited tourist spot. The deck here is unusual in that its surface is built at a slant so water can run off. Less visited, but magical, is the deck around the back of Daikakuji that overlooks an old lake where nobles used to go boating and poetry-writing at night. Thinking back to our nights reciting Chinese poems on David Kidd's moon-viewing platform, it makes me wonder if we read poems for the same reason that the Daikakuji courtiers wrote them. Just as a *tokonoma* practically forces one to set up a flower arrangement, a moon-viewing platform compels one to read or recite poetry. The deck was making us do it.

How to Walk and Talk

Cultures that take off their shoes and live on the floor develop a cult of how to walk. I think there might be two reasons for this. First, with bare feet or only socks, you can slide along a floor, and there are lots of interesting ways to slide. With shoes, you can only stomp. A second reason might be that with people seated on the floor itself, their eye level is closer to the feet walking near them, so they'll take more notice of the movements of heels and toes.

In Indonesia, court nobles slide and glide their feet in a certain way. That gets into court performances and is one reason for Javanese dance's ineffable elegance. In Japan, Shinto priests shuffle their feet along wooden decks, and that sacred movement has filtered into Tea ceremony and Noh drama. You can slide better when you're wearing socks than with sticky bare feet, so *tabi* took over and became de rigeur. If you brush your *tabi*-ed feet together while walking, they make a particular sound, a cross between a whoosh and a squeak, a kind of whish. That sound is much valued in the Tea ceremony. So you need to pay attention not only to how your walk looks, but to how it sounds.

In Thailand, where buildings on high stilts had floors that were not joined as tightly as they were in Japan, there was much concern about noise. Children were taught to walk slowly and lightly so as not to make the floors creak, and from that derives, in Thailand, a cult of gentleness—keep your voice low, close the door quietly, and be gentle with people and things. A waitress in Thailand would never slam a plate down on the table like you might see in China.

Neither would a Japanese waitress. It's because the Japanese, too, developed a cult of how to walk, and that's because of the floors they walked on.

Goeido hall of
Higashi-Honganji temple

Chapter 5

Tatami

畳

Tea ceremony and flower arrangement
take the shape they do because of tatami.
But before tatami was wood, mud, and sand.

fter the communist victory in China in 1949, David Kidd fled China and went to New York where he worked for the Asia Society. There he met the young Sen Soshitsu, who was then in his twenties, still just the heir apparent but later to become the 15th Grand Master of Urasenke Tea. David longed to live in Asia, but could not return to China, which remained mostly closed to outsiders and roiled by Maoist turmoil until the late 1970s. Soshitsu invited David to come and live at Urasenke's headquarters in Kyoto, and he jumped at the chance. So David came to Japan, in his view second best, but as close to China as he could get.

David arrived in Kyoto on Christmas Day of 1952, and this was a Kyoto that none of us has seen. The city was still intact, looking as it had for centuries, before the postwar process of tearing down the old city and replacing it with concrete boxes had really got up and going. Snow was falling on tiled roofs stretching out in all directions; wooden doors and shutters, faintly seen through a misty chiaroscuro of snow, beckoned from tiny lanes. It was pure magic, and David fell in love.

The love affair did not last long. David lived inside of Urasenke for about a week until one day they told him that he couldn't step on the cracks of the tatami. David moved out the next day.

Life on Tatami

That, of course, is Chinese mentality. You don't tell a Chinese where to step, but you do tell a Japanese. And it's determined by the fact that you have tatami. An open wooden floor is just a clear space; it's boundless, it has no levels, no way of knowing what's higher or lower, and you cannot, just by looking at it, measure its size or proportions. Tatami, with their clearly marked edgings, tell you instantly that this is a four-and-a-half-mat room or an eight-mat room. There's an exact sense of space.

What happens next, which I think is very human, is that because tatami had edgings, people came up with the idea that you shouldn't step on the borders. It's the mentality of "Step on a crack, break your mother's back." In order to walk gracefully—while never stepping on a crack—Tea ceremony developed rules as to which foot to start on: Urasenke Tea starts on the right, and Omotesenke Tea starts on the left, and so on.

It was only in early Edo that tatami covered most indoor spaces, and from this time on, people's behavior changed. It would never have occurred to anyone to come up with these forms of walking with open wooden floors. So tatami have led to a mindset.

In psychology they speak of "compulsive behavior," in which a person becomes addicted to a specific act, or series of acts, which are always repeated and must never be changed. Like don't step on the crack, or you must always walk around the block once before climbing the steps to your home. We all develop compulsions. It's not unique to the Japanese. Not stepping on the cracks in the sidewalk is built into our inner souls. For some reason it's irresistible, avoiding those cracks. Even if no one ever told you not to step on the crack, you probably wouldn't.

But in Japan, compulsive behavior goes much further, and I think it's because Japanese society, especially Kyoto society—hierarchical, inbred, focused on itself, aristocratic, and for centuries at peace—was a fertile breeding ground for repetitive detail. Compulsive behavior was constantly reinforced and refined, until it became art.

There's an entire choreography of how the Tea ceremony guest walks in the room, how the host enters and leaves the room, and how you advance to pick up the tea and retreat to bring it back. Every step forward and backward is determined so that the timing will be exact, not only to avoid the crack but to cross the crack on the correct foot depending on which school of Tea ceremony you adhere to. The Russian ballet never came up with fancier footwork. Tatami determine behavior. So when you look at a lovely tatami-matted room in Kyoto, it's not, "Oh, what a nice tatami-matted room!" It's actually, "Oh, what a nice tatami-matted straitjacket!"

―――――

Some Modules Are More Equal than Others

Actually, when you're counting tatami as a guide to floor area, they can be misleading. Tatami are based on the distance between two pillars (a *ken*), and it turns out that not all *ken* modules are the same. Nowadays Japan has three such modules. The first, called *Kyo-ma*, "Kyoto space" (or *honken-ma*, "true space," because it

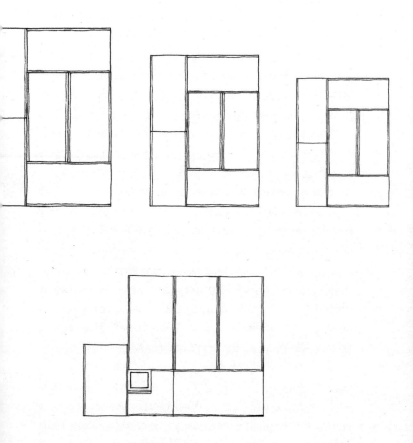

Top: *Kyo-ma*, *Edo-ma*, and *danchi-ma*, the three sizes of tatami

Bottom: Tearoom with a small *daime* tatami

was the original one), is used in the Kansai area and farther south down to Shikoku and Kyushu. Meanwhile, in the Kanto area centered on the city of Edo, they came up with their own measurement of a *ken*, called *Edo-ma*, and it was a few centimeters shorter than in Kyoto. That makes an *Edo-ma* tatami about fifteen percent smaller than *Kyo-ma*. In recent years *Edo-ma* has spread throughout Japan, and today it's close to being the national standard.

So six mats in new Tokyo are not the same as six mats in old Kyoto. But people are not yet in the habit of thinking in terms of square meters. They still visualize the size of a room by how many tatami it contains. Real estate developers cottoned onto this and came up with an even smaller size of tatami, called *danchi-ma* "public housing space," or *apato-ma* "apartment space," which is only eighty percent the size of *Kyo-ma*. A home purchaser in a new condo can feel content that he's living in a ten-mat room, even though it would only be eight mats in Kyoto. So tatami in modern apartments are deceptive and have been used for nefarious ends.

In a different way, the tea masters played with the rules by coming up with, for example, a small space that was not quite as large as a full tatami. A fraction of a tatami. They called it a *daime*, and it could be done with either wood or a specially ordered mini-tatami. You could have a tearoom of *ni-jo daime*, "two mats and a *daime*."

The *daime* was liberating because it allowed for irregular, quirky spaces. But it was also a case of the tea masters being a bit contrary and ornery, because the *daime* messes up perfect *ken*-based dimensions. In order to accommodate a *daime*, the tearoom has to be off center, or have a window box added on. It must be built differently from the way buildings usually are—and to have conceived something a little bit different was exactly the fun of such a design.

Limination at Work

All of this connects to the principle of Limination: drawing clear lines between times and spaces. As I mentioned when we were talking about gates and walls, limination applies to things like the seasons. There's a time when you're supposed to put on your thick sweater or your heavy silk kimono because the rule tells you that it is still winter even though it could be a warm spring day. People stick to rules like this because a line has been drawn.

This applies to the layout of a Japanese house. Think of the *genkan*, "foyer." You just can't have a house without a *genkan*. Even the tiniest apartment has one, if only two square feet in which to leave your shoes. The *genkan* has a distinct function that's not the same as any other, and it can't be left out. Similarly, the corridor, the hallway, the verandah, and the *tokonoma* are each clearly delineated.

What we see in the *genkan*, in the edged tatami, in the ironclad rule of *kamiza-shimoza* and so forth, is limination. Lines drawn between people and spaces. When you start drawing those lines it leads to a certain kind of behavior that then reinforces itself. That is, compulsive behavior.

If you've practiced long enough exactly which foot to put before the other and which line to cross or not cross and how, you develop a certain mentality. You become a different person from someone who strides freely across an open wooden floor without thinking about it. We sometimes say, "a man is what he eats," but we could also say, "a man is where he walks."

The Rise and Fall of Tatami Borders

Because they stood alone, Heian-style raised mats of the type that Emperors and princes sat on had brocade edges encasing all four sides. But once they started joining tatami together to cover a whole room, they only applied edgings to the two long sides of the tatami, and not to the short sides.

Sometimes, one needs to escape the relentless limination of tatami. There are spaces where you don't want to be bothered by the edging telling you too much. One such area is in a martial arts hall or *dojo*. Many *dojo* use tatami instead of wood because you need to be able to tumble on the floor when someone throws you or hits you over the head with a wooden sword. You need tatami for its softness. So the answer is tatami minus the edgings, which is what they typically use in *dojo*. These might be enormous spaces—there's one great historical martial arts hall behind Heian shrine where you can see this—hundreds of tatami, but no edgings at all. This allows the hall to be an open, undelineated space.

Otherwise you'd be prancing around like a tea master afraid of stepping on a crack, and you wouldn't survive one swat.

Limination has its limits. It turns out that there are a few ways to work around the dictatorship of edgings. It's in how you lay the tatami out. From this convention, one can lay out two types of rooms. In the standard one, called *shugi-jiki*, "formal layout," the tatami are laid alternately, some vertical, some horizontal. The edgings of the tatami allow us to measure a room at sight; we can see clearly that this is a six-mat or eight-mat room.

For larger rooms, however, they just line the tatami up in parallel rows. This is called *fushugi-jiki*, "informal layout," a striped effect of long horizontal lines, which makes it a little harder to get a sense of the overall area.

Tatami reached their epiphany, the grand finale of Beethoven's Ninth, in the vast matted halls of Chion-in, Nishi-Honganji, and Higashi-Honganji. What began with one raised mat in a Heian palace now exploded into immense communal spaces laid with hundreds of tatami. The main hall of Higashi-Honganji's Goeido, said to be the largest wooden building in the world (we've always been told that it was Nara's Todaiji, but actually Todaiji doesn't have quite the floor area), comprises over nine hundred mats.

Note, all three of these temples belong to *Jodoshu* (Pure Land) and *Jodo Shinshu* (True Pure Land), the two main sects of Pure Land Buddhism. Pure Land was a truly populist cult and its leaders were the televangelist

Square, borderless "Ryukyu tatami"

The two ways to lay tatami

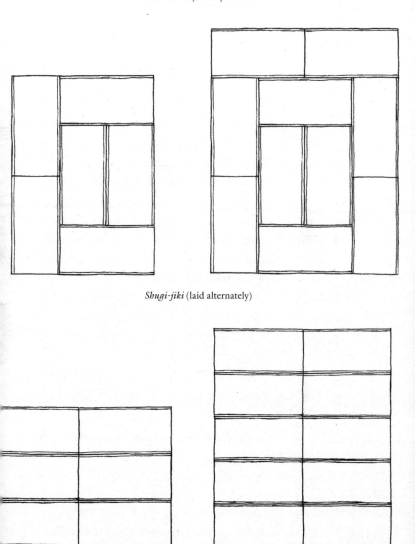

Shugi-jiki (laid alternately)

Fushugi-jiki (laid in rows)

preachers of their time. They were the first to bring the great unwashed public inside the temple and seat them in the thousands side-by-side under the same roof as their respective founders Honen and Shinran. With throngs of believers crammed in a multitude on a stretch of tatami that goes on forever, we've come a long way from the fine distinctions in rank that tatami once stood for. Chairman Mao famously said, "Serve the people!" The motto of Pure Land might be, "Seat the people!"

Those huge halls use the striped *fushugi-jiki*, "informal" approach of just laying tatami in rows. But why not get rid of edging altogether? The Ryukyu Kingdom (now Okinawa) had tatami without edgings, and today so-called "Ryukyu tatami" are sweeping the land. Compared to old-style tatami, they look fresh and chic. Not only don't they have edgings, they're only half the size of a normal tatami, making them square instead of rectangular so they're easy to move, and can be laid out in a checkerboard pattern. Ryukyu tatami are "tatami lite." You might very likely see them in a modern hotel's "Japanese-style" room, or in a renovated *machiya* townhouse. But never in an old temple of Kyoto. At least for now. Come back in a hundred years, and they might all be Ryukyu tatami.

―――――

Tatami and the Arts

Whatever you do, there's no escaping tatami because they are part and parcel of traditional culture. Tea ceremony, Ikebana flower arrangements—take away the tatami and you lose something. You lose quite a lot, actually. In Ikebana flower, which developed within the "frame" of the *tokonoma*, all those rules about "Heaven, Earth, and Man," and the angles at which branches and stems should be set, assume that someone is viewing the arrangement from floor level. Remove the *ikebana* from its alcove and raise it up onto a table, or display it in the wide-open space of a hotel lobby, and it takes on a new life. Freed of the *tokonoma*, it outgrows the restraints that used to govern it and becomes something new: modern art.

In the case of Tea, they invented *Ryurei*, "Raised Ceremony"—so-called because it's raised above the floor. The host sits at a table laid out with tea utensils, and the guests sit nearby on black lacquer stools, which are aligned in front of little benches where they place the tea bowls. Created in 1872 at an international exhibition for foreigners who couldn't sit on the floor, it's now a standard form of Tea ceremony with well over a century of history behind it.

Minimalist black-lacquered *Ryurei* furniture has a sleek appeal. It's convenient for social events where you have a lot of people coming through, as in Kyoto's *Miyako Odori* geisha dance, where the geisha serve all the guests a cup of tea in a room off the lobby of the theater. Many thousands traipse through the lobby every day, and if everyone had to sit down on tatami in a tearoom, the geisha's work would never be done.

Also, it's a fact that modern Japanese no longer live on the floor, and prefer chairs as much as Westerners. It's nice to be able to sit on a chair and not on the floor.

Or so you would think. But teetering on those minimalist stools with no backrests, you feel like you're sitting "at attention" the whole time. The Tea ceremony takes place in the middle of a room, so there's nothing to your back. There's no space to settle into. Without the tatami that frame the encounter, Tea seems naked; you can't close your eyes and let the dark and quiet mood of the tearoom carry you away. *Ryurei* works as a social event. But not as the meditation that Tea was meant to be. Like it or not, the arts of Tea and Ikebana were created on, by, and for tatami.

―――――――――

Earth, Lime, Sand, and Tile

In the previous chapter, when I was discussing wood versus tatami, I skipped an important part, namely the earthen floors that came even before wood. Japan's earliest dwellings from the prehistoric Jomon period appear to have been pit houses—holes dug in the ground with thatched roofs thrown over them, like a tent. Even after they shifted first to wood and then to tatami, Japanese houses went on having a part with dirt floors. It's called the *doma*, "earthen space," and is where the kitchen was.

Farmhouses sometimes feature huge *doma*, where, in addition to cooking, they used to keep livestock. While Chiiori had only a small *doma*, the old house where I live in Kameoka contained a very large one when I first moved in. The *doma* made up about one-third of the whole area of the house. In Kyoto, *doma* survive in many places, in temples as well as in *machiya* townhouses such as the historic Sugimoto-ke House. At Sugimoto-ke you can see a wide expanse of beaten-earth floor, lined with old-style cooking hearths and *tansu* chests.

This being Japan, even earth got special treatment. They developed a form of beaten earth called *tataki*, literally "three-mixed earth," so called because they mixed clay, lime, and brine to create what's sometimes called "Japanese concrete." The color, coming from red clay, is reddish or yellowish; it dries hard, and it's then oiled and burnished to create a smooth, shiny surface.

Tataki is a luxury. In an old farmhouse in the mountains, or at my home in Kameoka, the *doma* would just be pounded dirt. But in sophisticated downtown Kyoto, even the dirt must be polished. So they used *tataki* and it became the keynote for *doma* and entry foyers. You find many textures and colors of *tataki*. Once you've gained a taste for the unique material that is *tataki*, you start noticing it in the *genkan* of old inns, and in the kitchen areas at *machiya* townhouses and old temples.

Kyoto's ultimate earthen floor is located in a room, just to the right of the dais where the Emperor used to sit in the Seiryoden hall of the Imperial Palace. The room is called the *Ishibai-no-dan*, "Lime Altar," but it's nothing like an altar you would usually see in a temple or shrine. It consists of a five-by-three-meter space, at the same level as the wood-floored hall where the Emperor sat, but with a floor made of earth surfaced with a layer of polished lime. Except for that lustrous floor, and a screen along the wall, it is vacant. Here the Emperor prayed every morning, facing towards Ise Grand Shrine and the hall in the palace where they kept the "Three Royal Regalia" (the Mirror, the Sword, and the Jewel). From this earthen floor, the Emperor communed with his divine ancestors.

When the Emperor moved to Tokyo in 1868, the tradition of the morning prayers moved with him, and they set up a room in the palace in Tokyo that duplicated the function of the *Ishibai-no-dan*. But in Tokyo they carried on only the function, not the form; they didn't bother to re-create the earthen floor. Nothing like this would ever be built again.

In other palaces, notably China, the highest altar would be carved marble, gold lacquer, ceramic, or jade. But in Japan, they stripped away manmade refinements, and went back thousands of years to the Jomon period, when people lived in holes in the ground. Back to an earthen pit, basic and elemental, exerting an emotional pull as strong as Stonehenge. It's a mysterious place, and to my knowledge nothing like *Ishibai-no-dan* exists anywhere else. It's the "Floor of Power."

One would think that you couldn't carry floors to a more primitive level, but you can. One of the shrine buildings at Kamigamo shrine dispenses with floors altogether. Called Tsuchinoya, "House of Earth," it consists of pillars holding up a roof—sheltering nothing but an expanse of raked sand. It seems that its original purpose was simply as a place for priests to assemble before a ritual, but to my mind it's the best sand garden in Kyoto. It's pure constructions such as this that give Shinto its special sense of mystery.

In the Kamakura period, a new type of flooring

Kamigamo shrine's Tsuchinoya pavilion

Ishibai-no-dan, Imperial Palace

173

arrived from China: tiles, brought in as part of the new wave of Zen. Most of the palace and temple floors in China are tiled. The entryway to a Zen temple, and sometimes the entire floor of an initiation hall is laid with black tiles. In Kyoto, these tiles are squares made out of the same black earthenware that you see on roofs. They lay out these flat squares sometimes in diagonal patterns, sometimes in horizontal rows, and oil them to a rich blackness. That's the standard, but there are also paler tiles, gray verging on silver. So attractive, cool, and neat are these tiles that they expanded beyond *doma* and Zen halls, and now are used all over Kyoto for walkways and *genkan* foyers.

Coverings for Tatami

As for living spaces, tatami are not the last word. People also spread coverings on top of the tatami. The one you see most often is *mosen*, "felt." Felt was originally imported from Mongolia; it's light and soft, rolls up easily, and so it makes a convenient movable covering. Colored blue, black, or red, it comes in long rolls or in rectangles cut to the size of a tatami. *Mosen* are brought out for festive occasions, and people often lay *mosen* around the edges of a reception room, or on benches in a garden, to indicate where guests are supposed to sit. *Mosen* tells you it's a party.

One thing that you don't see so much in Japan is rugs on tatami, at least in "proper" traditional spaces. When you do see rugs, they're likely to be Persian, Chinese, or

Nabeshima rugs

Western-style ones. Who ever heard of Japanese rugs? Yet, this is something that you do find in Kyoto.

If you look at old paintings of samurai and literati, very often you will see them sitting by their desk on a small rug the size of one tatami, known as a *dantsu*. The *dantsu* were produced in the towns of Sakai and Ako, as well as Nabeshima fief in Kyushu, but Nabeshima *dantsu* were the most famous, so people ended up calling such rugs generically Nabeshima.

They got the techniques from Ming China, and many of the designs are Ming as well. Typically blue-and-white (with patterns similar to blue-and-white ceramics), these rugs spread all over Japan during the Edo period and were used in many different spaces. But as traditional living has faded in most towns outside of old Kyoto, many Japanese would now not be familiar with Nabeshima. I remember going to a Tea ceremony decades ago in Kyoto and being surprised that the guests sat on rugs. I had never seen them, but later I began to notice the rugs in paintings, and in traditional Kyoto houses.

And there's more. Floor coverings don't stop at textiles. In Kyoto they also use *shibugami*, which is thick, durable mulberry paper with a shiny surface. They dye it with *kakishibu*, "persimmon juice," the tannin giving it a deep purplish-brown color. At Sugimoto-ke townhouse, they spread broad sheets of *shibugami* several mats wide over the tatami in summer to create a sense of coolness.

Another popular floor covering is *toh*, a kind of wickerwork, basically rattan, that's woven into wide mats. Being water-resistant, it's the flooring that you used to see in bathhouses. It doesn't usually appear in living rooms, but because *toh* is quite tough, sometimes people lay it down to protect the tatami in areas with a lot of visitors, or in places with a lot of furniture and *tansu* chests.

———

Squeaking and Bleeding Floors

There are some floors in Kyoto that are truly objects unto themselves, transcending the buildings that they are in and the materials they're made of. The star case would be the famous squeaking "nightingale floors" of Nijo Castle that were designed to give the alarm if an intruder tried to enter. There are many items of interest in that palace, but if you were to ask the average Japanese high-school student or even ninety percent of adult visitors of any nationality what they remember the most about Nijo Castle, they'll talk about the squeaking floors. To this day those floors are carefully maintained, tuned like a piano by the people who look after Nijo. Flooring nails rub against clamps attached to the underside of the floors, and that's how the squeak is made. You can find squeaking floors in other places such as the corridors of Chion-in temple, but the one that remains in the best musical form is at Nijo.

Not all the floors to be found are under your feet. There's a group of six ceilings in Kyoto made from old floorboards known as the *chitenjo*, "blood ceilings." All five are connected to the same historical incident. After Hideyoshi's death in 1598, Tokugawa Ieyasu took over his castle at Fushimi, and fortified it with two thousand troops under his loyal retainer Torii Mototada. In 1600, when spies revealed to Torii that a massive force of Ieyasu's enemies was about to raid the castle, Torii bought crucial time for his lord by choosing to stay put. Greatly outnumbered, he led his defenders in a suicidal last stand. This sacrifice enabled Ieyasu to advance westward; a period of fierce warfare ensued, which resulted in Ieyasu's victory and the founding of the Edo Shogunate. But during those months, the bodies in Fushimi Castle lay where they fell, and their blood soaked into the wooden floors.

Ieyasu's grandson eventually tore down Fushimi Castle and donated the floors to a number of temples in and around Kyoto, who made the wood into ceilings out of respect for the spirits of the loyal departed. (Of these, three of the most striking ceilings can be seen at Yogen-in, Hosen-in, and Genko-an.) The ceilings are a favorite of teenage boys who visit in high-school tour groups, and many go away mistakenly thinking that warriors committed suicide and the blood shot up to the ceiling. That's not so. These are floors that became ceilings.

—————

Looking Up Rather Than Down

Speaking of ceilings, since we've looked down at our feet, let's look up at what is over our heads. Ceilings can tell us as much as floors about the purpose of a place. In Nijo Castle and Shugaku-in Detached Palace, which feature different levels of floors, the ceilings above them rise or fall in different levels as well. Usually, as the floor goes up, the ceiling goes up too. However, there are times when there is no change in floor level and only the ceilings vary. In any case, the ceiling is telling you who sits where.

In the oldest farmhouses there were no ceilings as such. They were open all the way to the thatch with exposed roof beams. That is still seen in the *doma* earthen areas. In Kyoto, *doma* kitchens are high and airy, soaring up to two- or three-story-high atrium-like spaces with big, naked roof beams above.

But those soaring big *doma* spaces are notoriously dark, as the dim rays from candles or lamps die out in the gloomy upper rafters. Plus, all the heat rises up to the roof, leaving the floor level freezing cold in the winter. So aside from *doma*, most rooms, even in farmhouses, have ceilings.

Ceilings in your normal Japanese-style house are usually thin planks that hang from a framework suspended from the rafters above. In grander places, you find a kind of coffered ceiling known as *gotenjo*, which grew up in palaces. Like so many things, I believe the idea came from China. A coffered ceiling is made up of slats of wood that crisscross, creating squares. Sunken into each square is a piece of wood. Reserved for nobles or shrines, coffered ceilings date back to the Heian period.

You can see an old form of it in the pavilions outside the main part of Kamigamo shrine. Some of the finest court-style architecture in Japan is there. The Emperor and the noble emissaries to the shrine would temporarily reside at these pavilions as they came and went. The pavilions were built with no walls but otherwise they are miniature palaces, and you can sense from these what a true ancient Japanese palace would have been.

Note that the ceilings at Kamigamo also arch upwards at the edges. This is called an *oriage-tenjo*, "upturned ceiling," and adds even more cachet. At Nijo Castle, the entire ceiling of the main reception room is *oriage-tenjo*, but it divides into two sections: a lower ceiling over the area where visitors and attendants sat, and a higher one over the *jodan-no-ma* where the shogun held court.

Above the mats where the shogun sat, the ceiling rises yet again, creating a small third level. It's a *niju-oriage-gotenjo*, a "double upturned coffered ceiling," reserved only for a supreme lord.

The space between the lattices in *gotenjo* ceilings can be as large as fifty centimeters on each side. In Momoyama and Edo palaces, every flat surface was decorated, and so the coffers often got painted as well. Nijo Castle once had elaborate paintings on the *gotenjo* in the corridors, but they were damaged in early Meiji and got repainted rather clumsily. So in Nijo Castle you should definitely look down, not up. But in some side passages of Nijo, not the main corridor, original paintings on the *gotenjo* are still preserved.

One tends to focus on wall paintings, but there are also ceiling paintings. They usually portray mythical subjects like phoenixes and dragons. I think it's because they are animals of heaven, and the ceiling is the sky. In large temples, the ceiling became one huge wooden canvas. The most spectacular example of that is at Myoshinji. The enormous dragon on the ceiling by Kano Tan'yu

Niju-oriage-gotenjo, "double upturned coffered ceiling," at Nijo Castle

181

was painted so that no matter how you look at it the eyes seem to follow you.

Inventive Tea Ceremony Ceilings

Tea masters began to play with the materials of the ceilings just as they played with the flooring. For example, as part of the vogue for things that reminded them of farmers and fishermen, they favored a *funazoko tenjo*, "boat-hull ceiling." A *funazoko tenjo* rises up on two sides to a ribbed peak in the center. The concept, as I've heard it explained, is that you have turned a boat upside down and you're living under it. Supposedly when the earliest Japanese arrived on the beach from the Pacific Ocean they turned their boats upside down, put them on stilts, and lived under them as their first dwellings. I think that is an old wives' tale, but in any case a *funazoko tenjo* was considered rustic.

In addition to *funazoko tenjo*, tearooms would also have ceilings made of woven bamboo or cedar strips. Or a combination of these. There's a bewildering variety of tearoom ceilings, each with its own name, such as *ochi-tenjo*, "dropped ceiling," for a low ceiling over the place where the host sits; *kakekomi tenjo*, "propped-up ceiling," for a ceiling coming off at a diagonal; *takesao tenjo*, "bamboo-pole ceiling," for ceiling planks held in place by bamboo; and *kesho-yaneura*, "decorative underside of the roof," for a ceiling that uses the roof structure itself as a design motif. In Tea it's thought to create a countrified impression because it doesn't hide the roof—just as one

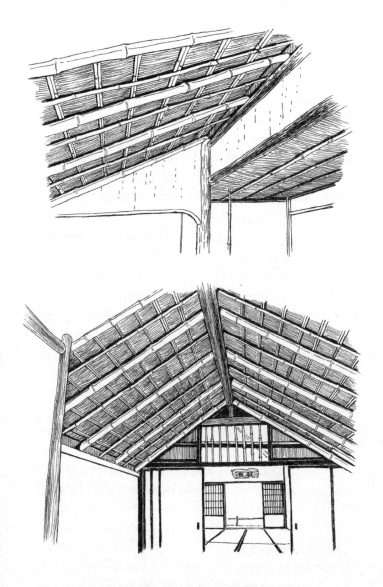

Top: Tearoom ceilings in two levels
Bottom: *Funazoko tenjo* at Katsura Detached Palace

might see in an old farmhouse. By combining different woods in roof sections, some flat and others sloping, the room could be divided into two or three partitions without ever breaking up the floor plan. In a tearoom, you need to look up as well as down, because the ceiling is telling you, if the floor doesn't, where you can sit and what kind of room this is.

Beyond hierarchical concerns, the ceiling might also be reminding you of living in a farmhouse, of being in a homey unaffected space.

You could say that tearoom ceilings are the architectural equivalent of haiku—intense creativity applied to a surprisingly limited basic form. The range of ceilings found in tearooms is a reminder of why Tea ceremony is endlessly fascinating. Ceilings that rise, descend, or slant, made from every variety of wood and bamboo. Tea masters used the ceilings to indicate the positions of host and guest, or to instill a sense of bucolic charm, or sometimes just to show off an amusing new architectural idea. The creativity lavished on these ceilings is remarkable—so, although they usually only tell you the part about admiring the *tokonoma* when you enter the tearoom, it's also worth it to give a glance upwards. The ceiling might tell you far more than the *tokonoma* does.

―――――――――――

The Cult of the Floor

If the ceiling signifies sky, the floor can be seen as a garden. Sometimes temples array flowers on the floor as an offering to a Buddhist statue or altar. I've seen this done

Flowers on the floor at Honen-in

at one of the subtemples of Myoshinji and also at Honen-in's main hall. They place a few large flowers, such as orchids, camellias, or chrysanthemums one by one on the floor, arranged in rows. You can see that the floor has eroded slightly at these points from the moisture of many years of dewy flowers. Expanding rows of big flowers on the floor—like rays of light emanating from the Buddha looming up in the distance: it's an evocative image, stronger than any arrangement of branches in a vase.

So, Kyoto developed quite a cult of flooring. Sadly, a lot of this variety is lost when designers sit down to create modern versions of Japanese architecture. Because they've got it into their heads that a floor is made of tatami. That's the look of most modern *wafu kenchiku*, "Japanese-style architecture." Just add tatami, and presto, it's "Japanese."

We know that in fact there's also dirt, *tataki*, polished lime, tile, wood, and rug-like coverings. The *tataki* comes in colors from red to gray; the tiles can be gray, silvery, or black, glossy or matte, and laid horizontally or diagonally. If you wanted to go avant-garde, you could do a floor of raked sand like the Tsuchinoya pavilion at Kamigamo shrine.

The wood can be white *hinoki*, lustrous reddish *aka-matsu* or *tsuga* pine, strong-grained orange *keyaki*, and others, on down to industrial *sugi* cedar. It can be polished to a mysterious reflective black, or coated with red lacquer. It can be tuned like a musical instrument, or bedecked with flowers. On top of the wooden boards you can lay soft *mushiro* rice-straw or smooth *goza* mats, or tatami which combine the good qualities of both of these.

You can mix full-size tatami with fractional-size *daime* niches as the tea masters did. Spread over the tatami, there can be a set of blue-and-white Nabeshima rugs, rolls of blue or red *mosen* felt, squares of maroon *shibugami* paper, or a stretch of woven *toh* rattan. The idea that a Japanese room must be a bland expanse of standard-size empty tatami has led to a sterile, soulless feel in many modern Japanese-style interiors. Some Zen monk should walk up to these architects and shout, "*Kan-kyakka!*"

Roland Barthes, a modern French philosopher, wrote a small but very influential book about Japan called *The Empire of Signs*. It's very French, somewhat thin on content perhaps, but written with great authority. Nevertheless, I have to give Barthes credit because he had one big idea that really applies. And that is that Japan's culture is all about symbolism. The open and closed mouth of the *Ah* and *Un*, the rules of *kamiza* and *shimoza* that define the protocols for proper seating—there are endless examples.

As Barthes sees it, we're dealing with coded language. You're surrounded by symbols that are telling you something, and if you can't decipher the code, you'll never figure out the meaning or purpose of what you are looking at. It might be a pretty room, but unless you can pick out the telltale signs that indicate what's higher and lower, and who should be here and who shouldn't, then you simply won't know what your next step should be.

Dai'ichi-gi (第一義), "The First Principle,"
by Kosen, Manpukuji gate

Chapter 6

Plaques

額

Visitors at a Zen garden wonder,
"What could this mean?"
The answer is on a plaque hanging over their heads.

I n the 1960s I studied number theory in a summer program at Ohio State University under a brilliant but eccentric professor named Dr. Ross. Dr. Ross used to jump up on his desk and shout at his students: "Look deeply into simple things!" In that spirit, let's see how a simple and apparently obvious thing like kanji has impacted the city.

The Power of Kanji

Chinese kanji date back thousands of years. They are "ideographs," that is, each symbol stands for a word or an idea, and isn't made up of letters put together, as happens with alphabetical scripts. Other cultures like the Mayans and Egyptians had hieroglyphics like this, but all the others disappeared and alphabetic systems had the last word everywhere except in the Chinese cultural sphere. That sphere once reached from Vietnam, through China, Korea, Manchuria, and all the way to Japan.

In the 20th century, Korea and Vietnam dropped the use of Chinese kanji. So today there are only two cultural areas that still use ideographs—the Chinese world, which includes not only the mainland, but also Singapore, Taiwan, Hong Kong, and Chinatowns all over the place—and Japan. Yet that's close to two billion people.

Kanji are psychologically, profoundly different things from alphabets. Instead of lining up letters to create a sound from which you derive meaning, an ideograph is a discrete symbol that means something by itself. Even before it's a sound, a kanji is a word, and it jumps right into the brain in a way that alphabetical constructions just don't. Our modern equivalent would be the emoticons and stickers used in texting. When you open your iPhone messages, and you see that someone has sent you a sticker of a lonely bear dropping a single tear, it speaks worlds. To type a sensitive response, you'd have to use quite a few alphabetical letters to get across the same mood as that little bear.

Because it carries with it so many levels of history, each kanji is surrounded by a radiating rainbow of meanings. It stands for something that is larger than just a normal word.

Take, for example, the character 心, which in Japanese is *kokoro*. It can mean heart, mind, the core or center of something, love, intention, desire, or purity. Combine such kanji into certain expressions, and they take on a profundity that is never going to be found in alphabetic languages. So, personally I find it sad that Korea and Vietnam have cut themselves off from this culture with which they had a two-thousand-year connection.

Actually the Japanese language is ill-suited to kanji, since it's agglutinative. It consists of a lot of syllables strung together, piling up more and more syllables to add extra layers of meaning. That's totally different from monosyllabic Chinese, which does without tenses, plurals, and conjugations. So kanji were a bad fit. One scholar wrote, "It's Japan's tragedy that the Phoenicians didn't get here first."

It was basically impossible to write Japanese just with kanji, so they invented not one, but two sound-based syllabaries to make it work. That's why Japan now has this writing system, which is perhaps the world's most complex, stirring up kanji and the two syllabaries into one huge cumbersome mix.

Despite the difficulty of using them, kanji are here to stay. Not that there haven't been attempts to do away with them. The 18th century nationalist thinker Motoori Norinaga (1730–1801) tried to scrap kanji and wrote in an "Ur-Japanese" of his own creation, using only old Japanese sounds and avoiding anything that came from Chinese. It would be like trying to write English without any Latin- or Greek-based words, only using ancient Anglo-Saxon. Even when Norinaga's texts displayed the kanji from which he derived his alphabetical readings, the result was more or less gibberish.

As early as 1866, the shogun received a petition entitled "Proposal to Abolish Kanji," and by the late 1860s there was a move to get rid of not only the kanji, but even the two Japanese syllabaries, and to write everything in roman letters. They set up the Japan Romaji Society, which still exists today, but the movement never got far. It was too late. Kanji carried too much cultural baggage—centuries of poetry, history, and philosophy—to be cast aside.

Think of the mystique we associate with ancient Egyptian hieroglyphics, and imagine that we went on building pyramids and carving mysterious inscriptions on the walls. Such is the innate power of kanji.

Kokoro (心) "Heart," by Alex Kerr

Plaques and Inscriptions

The earliest engravings in bone and bronze are merely "text," recording some simple fact like "Today, no rain." But very quickly the ideographs graduated to become symbols with mantic power.

You could use these symbols to name a palace or pavilion, such as "The Hall of August Virtue," "The Orchid Pavilion," and so on. The aura of kanji expanded further as they became used as abbreviations, whereby just one or two kanji conjured up a line of poetry, or a historical event.

For example, the word *ritsumei* (立命), used in the name of Kyoto's Ritsumeikan University, literally means "to stand on destiny." But a classically educated Japanese would know that behind these two kanji lies a passage of the 4th century BC Confucian philosopher Mencius, in which he declares that "he who fulfills his heart" (尽其心者) will "stand on his proper destiny" (立命也). Japan inherited the tradition of using a few kanji symbols to express powerful ideas, and built these into the fabric of the temples and cultural centers of Kyoto.

In China it went much further than in Japan in that the words are carved right into the landscape. If you travel to a great mountain peak or a famous waterfall you're going to find carved into the stone, in sizes large and small, calligraphic inscriptions added over the centuries by the people who have come and admired these places.

In time the Chinese came to label every hall, pavilion, and gate, and even rooms within the halls and gates. You find a hint of something similar in medieval Europe, such as at Oxford, where the doors to an ancient library are labeled "Nature" or "History." But in the West we didn't label *everything*.

The Chinese added philosophical comments or verses to the labels. Often you'll find a three-part array, with a horizontal plaque above the door, and a pair of vertical plaques attached to pillars at the left and right. Kong Demao, a sister of the last heir of the family of Confucius, who grew up in the vast Confucian Palace in Qufu and continued to live there for a few years after the communist takeover, wrote a wonderful memoir about growing up in the palace, and wandering from room to room and seeing these calligraphic plaques exhorting dwellers in this house to higher virtue.

I know that many foreigners who travel to China to see the gardens of Suzhou are disappointed because they find them to be just a bunch of crowded rockeries and pavilions that are just too busy to their modern eyes. What these visitors are missing is that those rockeries and pavilions are not made only to be seen, they're also to be *read*. Dozens of inscriptions along the walls conjure up a Confucian story, or a journey to the land of the immortals. But most foreign sightseers can't read them, and many modern Chinese can't either. So a traveler today gets maybe ten percent of the pleasure that a traditional visitor to those gardens would have found in them.

Writing on the Wall

In China, the balance might be ten percent beauty and

ninety percent literary allusion. Kyoto is the reverse, with visual appeal accounting for perhaps ninety percent, but there's an important ten percent that is written in the form of inscriptions. People gaze at an enigmatic garden in Kyoto and wonder, what is that raked sand for? What do those stones mean, and for what purpose did they make this garden in the first place? Yet, right over the doorway, in large characters brushed in gold lacquer, it says quite clearly what that garden is.

An example would be Daisen-in at Daitokuji. I remember being struck by the garden when I came as a twelve-year-old boy because the climactic part of the garden in the main courtyard consists only of two conical piles of sand. That's it, which is about as far as you could go on the scale of abstraction. It's haunting. It's wordless, or so we would have thought.

But it turns out that it's not so wordless because over the corridor looking out on that garden, there is a plaque saying *Nenge Den* (拈花殿), which means the "Hall of Twisting the Flower." It's not just an old plaque incidentally hanging there—Daisen-in takes these words as its main logo, inscribed on *goshuin* (red-sealed documents) that it provides to pilgrims. So the concept "Twisting the Flower" must mean something important for this place.

"Twisting the Flower" is short for the expression "Twisting the flower and making a slight smile" (拈華微笑), which refers to the story of the first transmission of Zen. The Buddha was lecturing on Vulture Peak, giving one of his sermons. Tens of thousands of his disciples were gathered before him waiting for his words of wisdom. But

Nenge Den (拈花殿) "Hall of Twisting the Flower," Abbot's Residence, Daisen-in, Daitokuji

Katsu! (喝) at the entrance to Daisen-in, Daitokuji

this time instead of launching into a long philosophical sutra, he simply held up a flower and twisted it, turning it with his hand. One among the gathered multitude gave a slight smile, and that was the transmission of Zen. That person had understood the wordless wisdom. The plaque is saying that this is what this garden is—a wordless transmission. But saying it with words, of course.

One of the core concepts of Zen is that of transmission; that enlightenment has been handed down from masters to disciples, along a direct line leading back to Bodhidharma, who brought it from India to China, and before Bodhidharma, all the way back to that first turning of the flower. Later, disciples in his lineage brought it to Japan. It has been transmitted for millennia, and this garden is transmitting it now. That's what this plaque is telling you.

Of course in Zen there's never just one viewpoint. On the way into Daisen-in, at the foyer, there's a large sliding door and on it is brushed one enormous character, "*Katsu!*" (喝), in very strong calligraphy. "*Katsu!*" is what the great Tang dynasty monk Rinzai screamed when he hit people over the head with a stick. It's a wake-up call, a shock word, like shouting "Hey!" into the ear of a sleeper. If "Twisting the Flower" is the meaning of the garden, then "*Katsu!*"—a jolt to the senses—is its purpose. It's written there on that sliding door, before you even get to the garden.

The Gate of Daitokuji

Kyoto abounds in inscriptions and I would like to talk about just a few, because once you start looking you find them everywhere. One inscription with many resonances is the large plaque hanging over the second floor of the main gate of Daitokuji temple. Like everything in Kyoto, the gate has been built and rebuilt many times, with the most recent rebuilding at the end of the 16th century. In the mid-1500s only the first floor of the gate had been built; the second floor was completed in 1589. This was the era when Toyotomi Hideyoshi ruled Japan and Sen no Rikyu, the founder of the Tea ceremony, was in the ascendant. It was Hideyoshi's patronage that raised Rikyu to the level where he could become the grand master of Tea.

With Hideyoshi's support, Sen no Rikyu's word became law. Rikyu's taste in tea bowls, tea scoops, tea-room layouts, flowers, and the rest of it still dominates the field today. Rikyu became a monk of Daitokuji, while still active as a secular figure. It was part of the tradition. The Tea ceremony had begun within Daitokuji and had at least a hundred years of history there before Sen no Rikyu codified it into what we now know. The first tea masters had been monks, and therefore it was considered right that Sen no Rikyu would also be a monk. To this day the grand masters of all the Sen houses study Zen at Daitokuji at some point in their lives. So, Daitokuji is intimately connected with the creation of and continuation of Tea.

Let's talk a little bit more about Daitokuji. Zen, when it came into Japan, took two main paths. Anyone who practices Zen even today can explore those two paths

Kin Mo Kaku (金毛閣) "Golden Hair Pavilion," main gate of Daitokuji

depending on their personality and their master. One direction is stark meditation. The other direction is aesthetics.

You can take both directions at once, and many Zen masters do. Although both aspects can be found in Zen monasteries everywhere in Japan, the monastery that focused the most on the aesthetic aspect was Daitokuji.

The greatest Zen calligraphies that were ever produced in Japan came out of Daitokuji, along with some of the most important ink painting, especially the super-abstract "splashed ink painting." The first tea garden is in Shinju-an, and in the graveyard behind it stand the tombstones of Kan'ami and Zeami, founders of Noh drama. The other subtemples of Daitokuji overflow with cultural riches, paintings by Hasegawa Tohaku, gardens by Kobori Enshu, and so forth. So prestigious was Daitokuji that the princely family of Konoe, first house among the *kuge* nobles, transferred their tombstones here in the early 17th century. Daitokuji is where the elite wanted to be, alive or dead. From this time, calligraphic scrolls by Zen abbots have been especially valued in the tearoom, and among them Daitokuji abbots take first place.

At the high-water mark of Daitokuji ascendance, Sen no Rikyu sponsored the building of the second story of Daitokuji's gate, and commissioned a plaque for it. It's in large letters, close to a meter in height, reading: *Kin Mo Kaku* (金毛閣) "Golden Hair Pavilion." Anybody who walks through Daitokuji can't help but see it, but nobody ever reads it. One might wonder what in the world that means.

But first, let's carry on with the tale of Sen no Rikyu.

In gratitude for Rikyu's donation, the abbot of Daitokuji had a statue of Rikyu placed right behind that inscription on the second floor. The problem was that the dictator of Tea may have been Sen no Rikyu, but the dictator of Japan was Hideyoshi, and when he realized that he would have to walk under that gate with the statue of Sen no Rikyu over his head, he was very unhappy; so unhappy that he ordered Sen no Rikyu to commit suicide.

As for the inscription: Monju, called *Manjusri* in Sanskrit, is the bodhisattva of wisdom, typically shown in China or in Tibet or Japan with a sword in one hand to cut through ignorance, and books or scrolls in the left hand. The "golden hair" refers to the mane of the magical lion which is the "mount," that is, the animal, ridden by Monju. What the plaque means is that when you enter through this gate, you seek to become the golden-haired mount of the "God of Wisdom," thus dedicating yourself to wisdom.

So there in three characters, *Kin Mo Kaku* (Golden Hair Pavilion), is explained what the whole temple complex of dozens of buildings and thousands of paintings and calligraphies and gardens is all for. This is a place devoted to "Wisdom," which in this temple is arrived at through aesthetics. So, says the gate, "Abandon all non-aesthetic thoughts, ye who enter here!"

———

Entsuji

Sometimes plaques tell you something unknown, or below-surface about the history of a place. The Zen temple of Entsuji, which features Kyoto's most perfect "borrowed scenery" garden, was built for Emperor Gomizuno'o. Once when I visited there I noticed a plaque over the main altar which reads, naturally enough, *Ent-suji* (円通寺). *En* means "circle" and *tsu* means "penetrating," from which derives the meaning "All-Penetrating." All-Penetrating is another name for the God of Compassion, Kannon. It sums up in two words the far-reaching power of Compassion, which we find expressed in multi-headed, multi-handed sculptures such as those at Sanjusangendo. Whenever you see the word *Entsu* you know that you are dealing with a cult of Kannon.

So far so good, but Zen temples don't usually favor Kannon, so why would Kannon be here? On looking at the seal and signature, it appeared that the plaque was written by Ingen, the Chinese Ming dynasty monk who came to Japan in the mid-17th century and established the Obaku Zen sect. I asked the abbot how this plaque came to be here, since Entsuji is not an Obaku temple. He said that Emperor Gomizuno'o was deeply influenced by Ingen and became his follower.

Ingen met with a huge welcome in Japan, from the Emperor and shogun, down to the monks of Myoshinji and other great temples. The reason lay first with his personal charisma, but it was also believed that Ingen knew the lost secrets of the Mings. One expression of Ming mystery was the fact that Ingen's Obaku Zen managed to combine Zen and the cult of Kannon. People saw this as quite exotic. Since the temple was built for Gomizuno'o, under Ingen's auspices, it was named Entsuji to honor Kannon. The spirit of Ingen—and one imagines, secrets of the Ming that Ingen transmitted to the Emperor—can be found here among Entsuji's moss and rocks.

———————

Myoshinji Daiho-in

An inscription may tell us more about ourselves than about the temple. I once went with close friends on a visit to Myoshinji. It was a charmed day. We went way inside Daiho-in subtemple and there was a lovely sunny garden where we sat and had tea. I noticed that near where we sat there was a plaque which read *Tendaihorin* (転大法輪), "Turning the Great Wheel of the Dharma."

The words refer to the name of the founder of Daiho-in subtemple (Tendaihorin Zenji), but the concept behind the words is not rare or special; it may be the most basic Buddhist idea. When the Buddha began his preaching, he started to "turn the great wheel of the dharma." Turning the wheel has ever after been a pious act in East Asia, and you can see it in action at Seiryoji temple in Arashiyama, where people turn a large hexagonal box filled with sutras, wafting the merit of the holy words into the air.

As an aside, the calligraphy of that plaque is in a peculiar style that was only used by Imperial family members. Those twisty curvy lines, alternatingly soft and crisp, are a giveaway for a prince or princess. When I got home and looked up the signature, I found that the writer was Princess Fushimi-no-miya Bunshu, who also happened to be a Buddhist nun. So not only the meaning of the plaques, but their writing style also tells you something.

———————

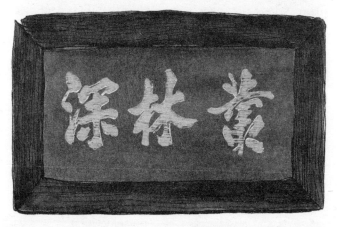

Top: *Entsuji* (円通寺) by Ingen, at Entsuji Middle: *Tendaihorin* (転大法輪)
"Turning the Great Wheel of the Dharma," by Bunshu, at Daiho-in, Myoshinji
Bottom: *Sorin Fukashi* (叢林深) "The Dense Forest Is Deep," Gesshin-in, Kodaiji

205

Kodaiji Gesshin-in

The other day I was involved in an unusual request. A Frenchman and an Italian woman who both live in Hong Kong came to Kyoto for a special dinner. She didn't know it, but he was planning to spring the question, and this was to be their engagement night. He asked us to set up a romantic dinner in a Zen temple, and Gesshin-in, a subtemple of Kodaiji, allowed us to hold it there. The full moon rose, and everything went well.

Just above the spot where they dined was a sign that the woman asked me about. It said *Sorin Fukashi* (叢林深), "The Dense Forest Is Deep." Dense forest, *sorin*, is a literary expression for a Zen temple. It means that you're in a place where there is more than meets the eye; there is something deeper, denser than viewing a nice garden—like getting an engagement ring.

Maybe I'm too suggestible. The thing about the plaques I've just mentioned is that they're completely general Buddhist slogans. There's no reason to take them personally. And yet I do. I think people in the old days did, too. You visit a certain place, with certain friends, at a certain time—and above you hangs a sign that gives that moment a name.

Plaques like these transcend the wall on which they hang. They're the whisperings of an oracle. They tell us more than the writer of the plaque ever intended. That's the power of words.

Urasenke Konnichi-an

Inspired by the rainbow aura of kanji, the Japanese took just as aggressively as the Chinese to naming every temple, hall, and garden. An example of a title for a room would be Konnichi-an, the main tearoom of Urasenke Tea Ceremony Headquarters. Based on this room, Urasenke itself took on Konnichi-an as an alternate name, and often when people speak about Urasenke they simply say Konnichi-an instead. *An* is a standard ending for an artist's studio and it means "thatched cottage," *konnichi* means "today." Konnichi-an is "Cottage of Today."

The story behind this is that when the grandson of Rikyu, Sen Sotan (from whom the three Sen schools of Tea descend), built the main tearoom of Urasenke, Sotan invited a Zen monk to come to the opening. By the time the monk had arrived, it was late and Sotan had gone, but he'd left a note for the monk saying please come back tomorrow. In reply, the monk wrote a note saying, "For this lazy monk, there might be no tomorrow." In short, there is only today. Sotan, impressed by the Zen message of valuing the moment, called the tearoom Konnichi-an, "Cottage of Today."

Manpukuji

Manpukuji is the richest source of these inscriptions that I can think of in Kyoto. It's close to China, having been founded by Ingen, the Chinese monk whose calligraphy we've already met at Entsuji. Ingen's thought and style became the rage of early Edo, and the shogun was moved to grant him land to establish Japan's third Zen sect, called Obaku.

Ingen built Manpukuji in Chinese style out of Burmese and Thai teak on granite bases that were carved in Beijing. The plaques, as in China, mostly come in sets of three, with a horizontal plaque at the top and pairs of vertical ones hanging along the pillars. Within Manpukuji there are four that I want to talk about.

We start with the front gate of Manpukuji, which features a tall central section with two wings on the side like Chinese decorative gates. Over the gate a brightly painted plaque reads *Dai'ichi-gi* (第一義), "The First Principle." It was written by Kosen, fifth abbot of Manpukuji, also a monk who had come over from China, and there is a little story about it. Kosen brushed the calligraphy once, but senior monk Daizui, who was standing nearby, said, "That's not the First Principle. Not good enough." Kosen wrote it again, and Daizui repeated, "Not good enough." This went on for eighty tries. Finally, Daizui left the room, and in a flash the abbot got it done. Daizui came back and said, "Yes, this is the First Principle. Good." This story is a Zen *koan*, an unanswerable question. Why would getting Daizui to leave the room be the right way to write a perfect calligraphy? Let's just leave that as a question.

Dai'ichi-gi, "The First Principle." It's telling you that Zen aims at something basic. Zen began as a means of cutting through all the complications of Esoteric

Buddhism with its long scriptures of hundreds of thousands of words, complex *mandala* images, multi-headed gods and goddesses, and so on. You were supposed to study these things slowly in stages, gain initiation, and then go on to higher things. But in Zen, they said, "Let's cut through all that. Instead of climbing Mount Everest in ten stages, let's jump straight to the peak." The founder of Zen, Bodhidharma, called it *Kyoge betsuden* (教外別伝), "A separate transmission, outside the scriptures," and he warned, *Furyu moji* (不立文字), "Don't rely on words." The idea was that Zen skips over logic and doctrine, piercing straight to that First Principle.

After entering Manpukuji's front gate, you pass through more gates, and there are inscriptions everywhere in Ming style. When you arrive at the founder's hall, there is a very large calligraphy which reads *Katsu-rogan* (瞎驢眼), "Eyes of a Blind Mule." When Rinzai, the 9th century Chinese founder of the Rinzai school of Zen, was dying, his disciples gathered around him and asked, "Oh, Master, what are your final words?" And Rinzai said, "You are all useless. Just a bunch of blind mules." And then he died.

The calligraphy was written by Hi'in, who had been Ingen's master back in China. Hi'in never came to Japan but sent this to his disciple Ingen, whom he had entrusted with passing on the Obaku tradition. The meaning of it is, "You're my top disciple, but is this knowledge really safe with you?" Hi'in is praising and criticizing Ingen at the same time.

The calligraphy has a clumsy lopsided look to it. In China, Hi'in had gotten into an argument with a Jesuit missionary about the merits of Buddhism versus Christianity and in the duel had lost his right arm, and so he wrote calligraphy with his left hand although he had been right-handed. Here we have a piece of calligraphy by somebody with a pretty fierce temperament who is struggling beyond his physical limitations to make a point. On his own part, by choosing to make use of this piece, Ingen is saying, "I am just a later successor in this long tradition and I'm nothing but a blind mule." His plaque is a commentary on the difficulty of passing down any kind of wisdom or talent to anyone. Yet it must be transmitted because Zen is very much about transmission. Another *koan*.

Proceeding on from the founder's hall, a bit farther up the hill, you come to the main hall, which houses a tall statue of Shakamuni. Behind it, in brilliant blue and gold, high over everything shining in the gloom, is a plaque on which is simply written *Shin Ku* (真空), "True Void."

That's the original Buddhist message—"All is Void." It's ultimate existentialism because there is no god, no salvation, no good or evil, and nothing means anything. There's only the "Void."

The temple complex rises slowly in a series of platforms with connected corridors. Finally, you arrive at the topmost hall. This is the Hatto, the Hall of the Dharma. There hangs my favorite of all the plaques at Manpukuji. It reads: *Shishi Ku* (獅子吼). *Shishi* is "lion" (again, Monju's lion, the vehicle of Wisdom); *ku* means "roar." "The

Lion Roars." This too was written by Ingen's master Hi'in. It's the message of Obaku Zen, shouting out from the highest point, cascading over those rooftops out to the world.

The fact that Ingen chose these odd, even freakish, pieces by Hi'in tells you something of why Obaku Zen had such charisma, and why its message resonates hundreds of years later.

As we know, scientists have been able to measure the temperature of the universe. It's the faint leftover or echo of the Big Bang twenty billion years ago. In that sense, within the quiet grounds of Manpukuji today, like hearing the ocean when you put a shell to your ear, you can still hear a trace of the roar of that lion.

So, those are the four: *Dai'ichi-gi* (The First Principle), *Katsurogan* (Eyes of a Blind Mule), *Shin Ku* (True Void), and *Shishi Ku* (The Lion Roars). Within the grounds of Manpukuji, you are being given a series of teachings, Buddhist lessons, merely by walking from front to back, and just by reading the plaques along the way.

One little story shows how importantly calligraphers viewed their plaques. The calligrapher Mitsui Shinna (1700–82) was commissioned to write a plaque for a temple in the Fukagawa neighborhood of Edo called "Edo Sanjusangendo." This temple had formerly been in Asakusa and had housed a statue of a Thousand-Armed Kannon. Accordingly, Shinna wrote a plaque reading *Entsu* (円通), the same kanji which Ingen had done for Emperor Gomizuno'o at Entsuji. But when the temple was moved to Fukagawa, they replaced the statue with

Left: *Shin Ku* (真空) "True Void," Daiyuhoden hall, Manpukuji
Top: *Shishi Ku* (獅子吼) "The Lion Roars," by Hi'in, Hall of the Dharma, Manpukuji
Bottom: *Katsurogan* (瞎驢眼) "Eyes of a Blind Mule," by Hi'in, Founder's Hall, Manpukuji

213

one of Yakushi (the Medicine Buddha). So now the new statue didn't accord with the inscription. Rather than rewrite the calligraphy, Shinna raised money on his own, and had a fresh image cast which was a Kannon, to match the *Entsu* on the plaque.

———————

Kanji Take Shape

It's not only plaques. Kanji express themselves in other ways in Kyoto. One example would be the gardens of Tenryuji and Saihoji, which are said to be among the oldest Zen gardens in Japan. At the center of each of these there is a lake which takes the shape of the character *kokoro* (心), "heart."

The lake is one giant kanji inscription, done in water and stone, rather than paper and ink. "Heart," which can also be read as "Mind," is a core concept of East Asian philosophy. The first thing that people trained in Buddhism might think of is *Kokoro wa jukkai o tsukuru* (心作十界), "The Heart Makes the Ten Worlds." This refers to the cycle of reincarnation, with the worlds of gods, starving demons, humans, animals, and other realms—but they're not really something that you die and are reborn into. They're already inside you; these worlds, they say, lie inside the human heart.

Zen references to the Heart (or Mind) are many and various. Asked "What is Buddha?" the Chinese patriarch Mazu replied, "This very Mind, this is Buddha" (即心即仏), and again, "Your own Mind, this is Buddha" (自心是仏). But in reply to the same question on another occasion, Mazu answered, "Neither Mind nor Buddha" (非心非仏).

Painting illustrating "The Heart Makes the Ten Worlds"

If you think that's confusing, consider another Zen master's answer to this question, which was "This is not Mind, this is not Buddha, this is not a thing" (不是心不是仏不是物). Such is the whimsy of Zen banter about Heart and Mind—all of which lies hidden, like shouts and murmurs rising from a sunken city, under the surface of those placid *kokoro*-shaped lakes.

In 1975 Tom Wolfe wrote a critique of contemporary art called *The Painted Word*. He argued that art had degenerated because it was no longer about pleasing the eyes; it had become just a way to express words—ideas and "isms" that art curators could argue about. Well, he would surely not have been happy with Zen gardens. Someone should write a book called *The Landscaped Word*.

━━━━━━━━

Daimonji

Aside from the Zen lakes, you find some other really big kanji. Notably *Daimonji*. One of the popular traditions of Kyoto takes place on August 16 at the time of the *Obon* festival, when six giant bonfires are set alight on five hills on the edges of the city. The event is called *Gozan Okuribi*, "Send-Off Fires on the Five Mountains." The biggest one is *Daimonji* (大文字), laid out in the shape of the character "big." It's exactly that, a huge *dai* (大), "big," spreading one hundred and sixty meters across, calligraphed on the hill with fire.

Hundreds of thousands of people come from all over Japan to watch the lighting of *Daimonji*. Of the other characters, on hills to the north and west, two are a pair, together reading *myoho* (妙法), "the wonderful dharma." There's also a *torii*, "gate," another *dai* known as *hidari* (left) *Daimonji*, and the outline of a "boat."

These bonfires are known as *okuribi* or "send-off fires," because the burning of *dai* and the other characters is part of the *Obon* festival in which the spirits of the ancestors come back briefly, are feted and remembered, and then sent off with lights, back to the other world. At the end of *Obon*, temples across Japan light lanterns, and some do big bonfires. Of these, *Daimonji* is the largest.

It commemorates a particular death, that of the son of Shogun Ashikaga Yoshimasa in 1489. This was the last in a long string of tragedies that befell Yoshimasa, not the least of which was the burning of Kyoto itself during the Onin War. We even know who the calligrapher of *Daimonji* is: Yoshimasa's mentor, the Zen abbot Osen Keisan. Although Osen should be better called "director" than "author" of the calligraphy. It's said that they draped strips of white cloth along the mountainside in order to display the draft of the character. Viewing from afar, Abbot Osen ordered adjustments to set its final shape.

Osen's eccentric Zen touch must account for why the character looks a little peculiar. But I doubt if one out of ten thousand people who come to see the lighting of *Daimonji* are aware of any of this. They're not missing much if they don't happen to know these scraps of historical trivia. The *okuribi* bonfires light the way for the spirits of *all* the departed, not just the shogun's son.

Ichiriki-tei

So far we've mostly talked about temples, but when you think of Kyoto's traditional shops, part of the ambiance is carved wooden shop signs, as well as *noren* (hanging banners) at the entrance, many featuring kanji in ingenious designs.

One *noren* that epitomizes this is the big one at Ichiriki-tei (一力亭) teahouse in Gion. Red-walled Ichiriki-tei, at the corner of Shijo and Hanami-koji, is Gion's biggest and most prestigious geisha teahouse, featured in Kabuki plays. The *noren* reads *man* (万) meaning "ten thousand." That's the number of tourists who pass it by every day, many stopping to peek inside and get a glimpse into the forbidden world of the geisha. Which is as close as they'll ever get because this *noren* banner, while just a piece of cloth fluttering in the wind, is as powerful a barrier as a steel bank vault door, separating forever those who can pay 100,000 yen for dinner with geisha, and the rest of us.

The *man* character here is a play on words because if you take the two parts of the character *man* (万)—"one" (一) on top, and "power" (力) below—it could be read as *Ichiriki* (一力), meaning "One Power." That was the name used in a popular Kabuki play, and eventually the shop changed its name to Ichiriki. However, Kyoto people sometimes still call Ichiriki-tei by its old name Man-tei (House of *Man*). It's a shorthand for insiders, based on a play on words found on the *noren* banner. Here the kanji is used with not much regard for meaning, but just for the fun of it.

Man (万) "Ten Thousand" banner at Ichiriki-tei restaurant in Gion

The World of *Bonji*

If you're on the lookout for interesting plaques, you sometimes find them written not in kanji but in *bonji* (梵字), "Sanskrit alphabet." One striking example is the big plaque, more than a meter square, that hangs in front of the five-story pagoda at Ninnaji. The writing on it appears to be just a bunch of curves and dots, unreadable if you're trying to figure out what the kanji would be. That's because it's not kanji; it's the *bonji* letter for the sacred sound *Aah*. Slightly different in shape from the *Ah* of *Ah Un*, "beginning and end," which we met earlier at each side of a temple gate, *Aah* stands for Dainichi Nyorai, the core Buddha of Esoteric Buddhism.

It's alerting you that this pagoda stands at the heart of this temple complex. The Cultural Agency thinks it's the Kondo at the top of the hill because it's much older. The Kondo is one of the less interesting buildings of Kyoto, but it has the distinction of having survived a lot of wars and fires. That impresses the academics. But the Ninnaji abbot who hung that "*Aah*" plaque on the pagoda knew better. With just one syllable, he's rooted us to this spot.

Two thousand years ago, Buddhist complexes began with pagodas. They were built to contain a sacred relic, like a tooth of the Buddha. Long before they raised temples to pray or meditate in, there were pagodas. From Southeast Asia up through China, the pagoda is the most sacred spot in a complex, the Mount Sumeru at the center of the quincunx. The pagoda is the part that points to heaven.

Aah (アーク) *bonji* (Sanskrit) plaque
on the five-story pagoda at Ninnaji

This plaque is a reminder that an alphabetic language actually reached Japan quite early, brought by India-inspired Buddhists. Texts written in *bonji* Sanskrit survived in 7th century Horyuji and many others were later brought over by China-traveling monks Kukai and Saicho in early Heian. Mostly they were inscribed on palm leaves, and they were unintelligible to average Chinese and Japanese except for a few elite monks. Add to this the fact that Indian philosophers had seen these sounds as sacred, as *mantra*, magic syllables. *Mantra*, in Japanese, translates as *Shingon* (真言), literally "True Words," which is the term used to refer to Esoteric Buddhism. So *bonji* acquired an untouchable mystique. They could never be used as a normal alphabet.

Bonji were called "Seed Syllables," because it was believed that each one contained the seed of a Buddha or bodhisattva. The mere utterance of one of these sounds conjured gods. A visual embodiment of this idea stands in the sculpture gallery behind Rokuharamitsuji temple in eastern Kyoto. It's a statue of the medieval saint Kuya, reciting the words *Namu Amida Butsu* (南無阿弥陀仏), "Glory to Amida Buddha," as he walks while clanging a gong. From his mouth emerges a wire from which spring six tiny bronze Buddha statues, a Buddha born from each syllable of the *mantra*. *Bonji*, giving birth to gods as they were uttered, gathered around them multi-hued clouds of meaning that alphabets don't usually have. *Bonji* became another kind of kanji.

The syllables of *Namu Amida Butsu* (南無阿弥陀仏), "Glory to Amida Buddha,"
become Buddhas as they emerge from the mouth of mystic saint Kuya, Rokuharamitsuji

Written but Unseen

The plaques of Kyoto are mostly invisible today. Most foreigners can't read kanji, and nobody can read *bonji*, so it's natural enough that they wouldn't see or notice these things. For modern Chinese and Japanese, too, the kanji are written in old forms that are not used now, or in cursive calligraphy that few can decipher, and even if they can read the words, the philosophical references are no longer known to them.

I've searched lavishly illustrated books of temples and gardens, and scoured the Internet to check out places where I know I have seen these plaques and inscriptions. Yet I hardly find a photo of any of them. They are forgotten, invisible.

Japanese ignore them not only because they're hard to read, but because they take kanji for granted. Kanji are hardly unique to Kyoto temples; they're a major part of the national language. In Japan, Kanji are the air we breathe. Those plaques may be inscribed in gold on red lacquer, yet they are not far removed from the prosaic messages—"No Parking" (駐車禁止), "Safe Driving" (交通安全)—that people walk by every day and ignore as a matter of course. Kanji plaques are submerged in a sea of triviality. Meanwhile foreign visitors and art experts glide blissfully over this aspect of Kyoto, because nobody brings calligraphies to their attention. So they remain just squiggles on wood or paper.

Of course the temples of Kyoto are not immune to the triviality outside their gates, and the premier instance of this is the prevalence—ubiquity—of advertisements for

Hitachi. For some reason the Cultural Agency has smiled on Hitachi Group's program of providing every cultural treasure in Japan with a sign that reads "Important Cultural Property, XX Temple or Shrine, HITACHI."

The other day I was viewing a Zen garden with some friends, and was primed to show them an especially enigmatic plaque facing the garden. But as we arrived at the garden's purest and quietest stretch of raked sand, a HITACHI sign standing right behind it caught their eyes. "Why Hitachi?" they asked, and there is of course no answer. It's a *koan*, a mystery as deep as the deepest Zen, and that must be why Daitokuji boasts dozens of HITACHI signs, and in Kyoto there must be hundreds. In many temples and shrines, HITACHI is the only word that non-Japanese are able to read because it's written in roman letters and not in kanji. So I guess, for foreign visitors, HITACHI is the most important plaque of them all. In the end, it's the message that they'll take home with them from Kyoto.

When one thinks about it, the proliferation of HITACHI signs springs, like traditional kanji plaques, from the ancient Chinese desire to label everything. What began as a "name" expanded into "poetry" and "philosophy," and has been transformed in modern times into "advertisement."

Wordplay

As it turns out, most of the plaques I've mentioned are found in Zen temples. In China, Zen was only a minor sect, and in the capital of Beijing temples took a back seat to the palaces of the Emperor and royal princes. So one doesn't find many Zen inscriptions in Beijing. But in Kyoto, Zen thrives, and with it, the wordplay of Zen monks. *Furyu moji* (不立文字), "Do not rely on words," warned Bodhidharma, but actually Zen is obsessed with words. That's what *koan* mostly are—wordplay.

The Zen monks shouted, "*Katsu!*" and challenged each other with quirky phrases—first they'd say, "Your own Mind, this is Buddha," and then they'd turn around and say, "Neither Mind nor Buddha." So they had it both ways, and you could never win an argument with a Zen monk. They installed enigmatic plaques at their worship halls and gardens, and brushed scrolls with pithy words of wisdom, by the tens of thousands. Those scrolls grace tearooms and *tokonoma* alcoves all over the city. It's words, words, words wherever you go.

Not only that, but the tradition of Zen eccentricity, and the idea going back to Rinzai that people need to be screamed at and slapped into enlightenment, meant that Zen calligraphies are strong and noisy things. By contrast, when a Chinese scholar sat down to brush an inscription for the garden, he did it with restraint. He might choose a refined antique script, savoring the elegance of each crisply written brushstroke. His characters have scholarly poise; they're reserved, even prim. So you can walk past dozens of them in a Chinese literati's garden and hardly feel the impact. Whereas Japanese Zen pieces are calligraphy turned up to high volume.

Big, rough, scratchy characters jab to the right and twist to the left, shouting at us, demanding our attention, refusing to be ignored.

As I mentioned earlier, people say that they find the rockeries of China "busy" and Japanese Zen gardens "restful." But it's quite the opposite. In the Chinese garden there's a place to stroll while chatting with a good friend under a stand of bamboo. There's a table in a pavilion to sit and have tea, and surrounding you rocks piled up here and there that make you think you're standing on a peak in the misty mountains or enjoying the fantastic scenery of Guilin. And after you've had another cup of this delicious tea, let's amble for a bit in the garden, shall we? But in Japan, you have to sit uncomfortably in one spot to behold the official view—a stretch of sand as forbidding as a lake of lava into which you wouldn't dare put one toe. Stern calligraphies warn you of what a serious place this is, and as for chatting with a good friend, you'd better keep quiet, or a monk might come and smack you over the head or shout "*Katsu!*" for not being enlightened enough. So much for restfulness.

One hears a lot about Zen silence, and the hidden mysteries of old Kyoto. But there's nothing silent, hidden, or mysterious because it's all written there, plain to see.

"Cloud Dragon" *fusuma* painting

Chapter 7

Fusuma

襖

With the advent of *fusuma* sliding doors, artists gained a huge canvas on which they learned to paint in new ways.

I n old civilizations if the cultural continuity goes on for long enough, you will have the classic situation of art copying life, then life copying art, and then the whole thing turning back around on itself. In 16th century Italy, sculptors aimed to capture the natural human body in marble. Their works set the standard for beauty, so that in 18th century France, the creators of ballet had their dancers pose in the ideal forms of Renaissance sculpture. In the 19th century, Degas then painted ballerinas in oil. And so it went back and forth.

In Kyoto this process happened with sliding doors.

From Dark into Light

The story begins with the fact that in Japan traditional houses had no walls. The only fixed internal walls that you typically find are at the back of the *tokonoma* alcove, or enclosing a work area like a *doma* (earthen-floored room, often the kitchen) or behind a closet. Inside the house proper, a *tokonoma* or a closet might not be more than two meters wide; the rest of the structure is just beams, pillars, and open space.

This is one of those points that suggests the Southeast Asian origin of Japanese houses. In Northern China and Korea, frigid winters called for solid walls of brick and plaster. But Japan's early settlers seem to have come from the south, and with them came the custom of building grass-thatched huts on stilts, with hardly any walls except maybe some woven bamboo.

Although Japan has freezing winters with snow and ice, for some reason they never adapted for that. They went on living for centuries in wide-open houses, as if they were still in the tropics. Anyone who has passed a winter in a traditional house knows what this means. David Kidd recalled watching old ladies in Kyoto, huddled beside a little *hibachi* (brazier) in a wide breezy room, rubbing their hands over the coals and politely murmuring *samuu gozaimasu ne* ("Cold, isn't it?")—with the doors wide open to the garden. "If they were so cold, why couldn't they just shut the doors?" wondered David.

Southeast Asian origin would seem to explain why Japanese architecture started out airy and stayed that way. However, there's another theory, which archaeologists favor, which says quite the opposite. Far from living in houses without walls, the earliest houses in Japan consisted *only* of walls. There was no airiness, only smoky darkness. First, people lived in caves, and later they built "pit dwellings." These were holes dug in the ground over which they propped up thatched roofs. It appears they climbed in and out via the roof.

Frankly it baffles me that people would choose to live in a hole in the ground in this humid climate. But archaeological evidence tells us that these were indeed Japan's first dwellings. In any case, as early as the 4th century AD we find clay models of houses with high-pitched roofs that look remarkably similar to the houses on stilts, with flaring "boat-shaped" roofs that you can still see in Indonesia.

Airy Southeast Asian-style houses and dark pit dwellings would seem to be totally at variance with one another, but it seems that at first, the two types of structures coexisted. It's thought that people lived in the pits while they built stilt houses above ground to store rice.

Over time they adapted these rice-storage buildings for human residence, and from the 5th century, they had

Open-sided Japanese room, Chishaku-in

got up and off the muddy ground. Pit dwellings gradually disappeared. In the stilt houses they put in wooden floors and verandahs, and from here it feels like we're in familiar territory. Houses start to look like the *minka* (traditional houses) we know today.

Nevertheless, David Kidd was on to something. People did in fact need barriers to block out winter weather.

The clay models of houses found in ancient tombs show heavy walls sloping down from the "boat roofs." The oldest farmhouses we can find today have thick thatched roofs with eaves drooping so low that they're not much different from a pit dwelling. The sides are almost entirely walled in with clay and wooden boards. Inside reigned an eternal darkness.

Even now, old *noka* (farmhouses) are dark. The thatched eaves reach far out, shadowing everything, and deep inside the house you huddle in the gloom around a smoldering *irori* (floor hearth). So darkness, not airiness, really is the starting point.

It turns out that the theory of Southeast Asian "airy" origins is not so simple. The post-and-beam structure, as found in its Southeast Asian homeland, was naturally open to the elements. But in wintry and stormy Japan, they needed to find a way to be open at times and closed at others, that is, to let in light and air when needed, and at other times to close up against the weather. This required movable doors and windows, and the engineering of these took centuries.

———

Sports-Car Doors

Along came civilization some time in the 6th century. Things Chinese began pouring into Japan. Farmhouses stayed low and dark, but palaces and temples got taller and larger. With the use of tiles rather than thatch, roofs got sturdier. Then came the first doors. We see Chinese

Pit dwelling reconstruction

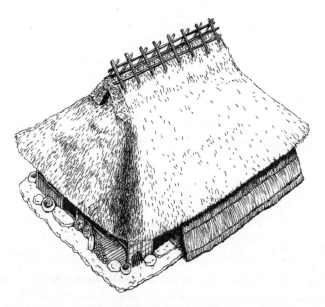

16th century farmhouse, with low eaves and walls of clay and wood

hinged doors with metal fittings at the temples of Nara, and also in the earliest surviving palaces.

From here on the homes of the nobility aimed for light. Light was the first luxury of Japan. Those who lived in the light had status and everybody else did not.

The first thing the builders of shrines and palaces came up with were *shitomido* (latticed doors). In contrast with a Chinese-style hinged door, which was one solid piece of wood, a lattice let in light and air. If you had the means, you could cover it with paper or silk. So far so good, but here's where Japan's taste for quirky engineering starts to show itself. Rather than hinge the doors on vertical pillars, like the Chinese and everybody else did, they came up with a counter-intuitive approach; namely doors that hinge above on a lintel, opening out and swinging upwards. They were like the gull-wing doors on the DeLorean sports-car, later turned into a time machine in *Back to the Future*.

Lifting up a huge *shitomido* that would be the entire height of a door was not practical. So most consisted of two parts: an upper set on hinges, and a lower set that don't swing, and can be pulled out and removed.

Builders attached the upper *shitomido* so they could be raised and hooked to hang open parallel to the floor below. I can't think of doors that swing open upwards anywhere else in the world. So prestigious were these first attempts to let in light that they became the mark of royalty. You can still see *shitomido* in Kyoto palaces and Imperially connected shrines.

Hinged doors at Sanjusangendo
Top: Detail of hinged door

Left: *Shoji*-lined exterior, Katsura Detached Palace

Right: *Shitomido* (latticed doors that swing upwards)

Once the form of the lattice was established, it was natural to paste paper on it. Slim down the heavy wood frets of the *shitomido* to make a more lightweight lattice, and you end up with *shoji*, sliding doors made by pasting paper onto one side of a wooden frame. Before these could appear, though, another piece of engineering needed to happen. The trouble with hinged doors, vertical or horizontal, is that they take up space. They swing into or over part of a verandah or room. The *shitomido*, meanwhile, were not very convenient, as the upper parts were heavy to lift up, and the lower parts had to be removed, carried somewhere, and stored when not in use.

———————

An Engineering Breakthrough

You could get around these problems by having doors that slide. It took hundreds of years, but by mid-Heian carpenters had cut grooves into the floor below and the beams above, into which they fit sliding doors. Seemingly obvious engineering insights like this are more difficult than they appear, as you can see from the fact that only the Japanese did it. The Chinese went on using hinged doors, and so did everybody else. Until the arrival of modern times, sliding doors were Japan's exclusive province.

Shoji, while not fully translucent like glass, let in light so they work well for external walls. But when you need more security than just flimsy paper—such as at night, or when you leave the house, or if a typhoon is coming—you can close up the house by using *amado*, wood-planked shutter doors that slide into place outside the *shoji*.

Amado are a remnant of the early dark days when the best people could do was to surround the house with wooden boards. *Amado* are temporary; their visibility in daylight hours is usually a sign that the house has been closed up tight and the owner is absent. With the *amado* retracted, sheets of white *shoji*, contrasting with the brown of the wooden columns and decks, define the exterior look of an old Japanese house. Slide the *shoji* open, and suddenly the whole structure opens up to the garden outside. Sunlight streams into the home; breezes blow through it.

Along the perimeter, *shoji* separate the house from, or open up to, the garden. But deeper inside, around living rooms and bedrooms, you need something that gives you more privacy than just a piece of paper pasted on a *shoji* frame. For these divisions, they came up with another kind of sliding door called *fusuma*. *Fusuma* are built with the same frame as a *shoji*, but covered with multiple layers of overlapping paper, creating a dense sound-absorbent padding, and over both sides are pasted large sheets of tough surface paper.

Shoji get children's fingers poked through them; they're fragile and need to be repapered regularly. *Fusuma*, on the other hand, are strong and semi-permanent. In the old days, you were supposed to repaper the *shoji* once a year; in contrast, a *fusuma* can last for centuries.

The *Shoin* Revolution

Sometime in mid-Muromachi, an architectural transformation took place. It's called *shoin-zukuri* ("studio" design). It was born as a way for the upper classes to show off their imported Chinese art works. A *shoin* (studio) consisted of a space with staggered shelves for displaying incense burners and other elegant objects. Next to this, there was a built-in bench by a garden window where you could lay out more objects, unroll a hand scroll, or brush a poem. The earliest extant *shoin*, Shogun Yoshimasa's retirement room, Tokudo (1486), survives at Ginkakuji.

After the simple layout of shelves and bench seen at Tokudo, the next stage in *shoin* design was to add a *tokonoma* (alcove) where you could hang scrolls. With *tokonoma*, there was now a niche for art.

I can't think of a similar development happening in China or Europe. In a Chinese palace or literati's studio, you could hang a scroll wherever there was free wall space. In a French chateau or noble estate in England, oil paintings festooned the walls everywhere. But in Japan, ever since the development of *shoin* with *tokonoma*, paintings were hung in the *tokonoma* and that was that. Maybe it was "limination" coming into play again, the irresistible impulse to put every object exactly in its place. If we're going to display incense burners, then let's put them on the official staggered shelves, and if we're going to hang scrolls, then let's hang them in the proper *tokonoma* "scroll hanging niche," and not just anywhere.

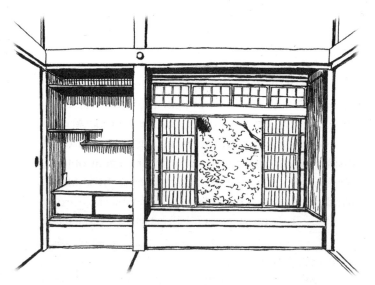

The *shoin* at Tokudo, Ginkakuji

Modern *tokonoma*

Since the purpose of *shoin* was to ostentatiously show off art works, it's a paradox that they are so *small*. The floor area of the *shoin* at Yoshimasa's Tokudo is just four-and-a-half mats, an incredibly spartan space for a shogun's retreat, even if it was built at a time of turmoil. Of course there were originally many more buildings in the Ginkakuji complex, now lost, in which we can imagine Yoshimasa living in luxury. But the spare and compact *shoin* suited the austere ethos of the times.

It also suited the limited budgets of the old aristocracy, who had been in decline since the fall of Heian in 1185. By the late 1400s when Tokudo was built, they were reduced to near poverty. A noble might have a few choice scrolls and incense burners to show off, but he couldn't afford much else. So a little *shoin* made the perfect combination of frugality and display.

The *shoin* pattern swept all before it and became the default for all later Japanese interiors. From this we get the *tokonoma* alcoves and decorative shelves we still see in Japan today.

Two other things happened in those *shoin* that are at least as influential. One is that they covered the entire floor, which until then had been all or partly done in wooden boards, with tatami. The other is that they started using *fusuma* to separate those tatami-matted spaces. From this time, *fusuma* came into their own.

Fusuma are not true walls, as they slide and can be easily removed. But they are fairly substantial, and their surfaces, consisting of great open stretches of flat paper, define the look of an interior. Which brings us back to darkness. Novelist Tanizaki Jun'ichiro in his famous essay *In'ei Raisan*, "In Praise of Shadows," picked up on the fact that Japanese houses are perpetually dark inside. Tanizaki argued that the dim interiors people lived in had created Japanese aesthetics. As a writer with a taste for sexual perversity, Tanizaki went on to explain how this even gave rise to the painted white faces of geisha.

Addiction to White

Darkness may be erotic, but not everybody feels like praising it. David Kidd used to complain about his home—which was a daimyo palace, so you'd think it would be bright enough—that living there was like swimming underwater. David said that, as he walked from room to room, he felt like he had to wave his arms around in front of him like a diver feeling his way through murky depths. In my work of restoring old houses I, too, find that it's always a fight against darkness. I want to add windows, wide glass doors, skylights.

The old Japanese didn't have those options, but they could brighten up their interiors simply by making them white. It was the natural thing to do, since paper covered their sliding doors, and paper is white. Also there was a long Shinto tradition of white as the sacred color. Folded white paper hangs from sacred rope; priests wear white; the vessels for offerings on the altar are all white.

Fusuma first appeared in Heian, in the houses of nobles, and they and the Imperial family were closely involved with Shinto ritual. So they covered all the *fusuma* in paper or white silk. There was even a late-Heian court manual that made a point of noting, "All the *fusuma* should be white."

If you think of China, you would never think of white. Red walls and orange columns, green and yellow roof tiles. But white really is the color of Japan. If we remember that light was the original luxury, it's natural enough that white would be thought of as "sacred" and as "high class." To this day, in Japan white is the standard for *fusuma* and walls, from the inner rooms of the Imperial Palace, to the interiors of restaurants, inns, and private homes. Japan has more white cars than any other color. Office buildings, corporate boardrooms, apartments all tend to be white.

White worked well in Shinto shrines and in traditional spaces where it was moderated by lots of wood and bamboo, and encased in deep shadow. And it was never pure white. One theory about Japan's "original white" is that it derived from bast fiber cloth, such as hemp or wisteria bark. Bast is one of those unusual, but wonderful words. It means tough fiber pounded out of bark or stems, rather than soft fibers spun from fluffy cotton flowers or silk cocoons. Washed many times in a flowing stream, the cloth woven from bast fibers bleached, and the light color and association with pure cold water led to the Shinto sense of white as sacred. Those early bast textiles were actually a kind of off-white with lots of impurities and variations. The same goes for white plaster walls. So the original Japanese white is actually a very complex thing.

In modern times white has become a misfit, a traditional concept mismatched with modern technology. Nowadays we can achieve pure white, which can be made to look even whiter by framing it in aluminum and chrome and bathing it in fluorescent light. The effect, far removed from the organic off-white of the old days, is sterility. This has not been to Japan's advantage, since architects or interior designers, when they want to create a posh impression, turn by default to this super-white approach. And we end up with bleak uninviting hotel lobbies of which there are plenty in Kyoto.

Addiction to white was one reason for the downfall of the high-end Japanese hotel industry after the 1990s. Within Japan, designers went on laying out sheets of white marble. But out in the world, Hyatt and Aman were experimenting with woody natural finishings, stone, bronze, indirect lighting, internal plants and gardens. When the international chains brought these concepts to Japan, travelers sought out the chic foreign-designed hotels and stayed away from the Japanese ones. Such are the perils of white.

Actually, there is another color that brightens things up considerably, and that's gold. If white is the color of Shinto, then gold is the color of Buddhism with its brilliant gilded altars. White meant "sanctified" and "sophisticated," gold meant "wealthy" and "gorgeous." While white was good enough for impoverished nobles in Kyoto, nothing but gold would do for the powerful warlords of the 16th century. It's said that all the *fusuma* of Nobunaga's Azuchi Castle were gold-leafed, which also made them reflect and intensify candlelight. Hide-yoshi had a tearoom covered entirely with gold leaf. Later, in the Edo period, when the newly enriched merchant class started purchasing folding screens, they too went for gold.

———————

Vast Canvases

With room after room lined with *fusuma* of white or gold, who could resist painting on them? I don't know when *fusuma* came into common use (Muromachi, or maybe earlier) but from that time on, they became the favorite canvas for classical Japanese painting. Many of the earliest remaining ink paintings that we have are not hanging scrolls but *fusuma* paintings.

Fusuma are quite large surfaces to paint on, so let's do the math to get a feeling for how large they really are.

The standard width between two pillars, or one *ken*, was 1.91 meters, and the height from floor to transom was 1.82 meters. There were two types of *fusuma*, a large size that was a full *ken* wide, and a narrow size, only half a *ken* wide. Now let's take a look at the central room in the main hall of an abbot's residence, called a *shicchu*.

Shicchu is not a very familiar word to most people, and it would seem to be a rather esoteric space, but if you go around Kyoto looking at Zen gardens, you'll see no end of *shicchu*. In fact, you'll often be sitting on the verandah of a *shicchu* as you look out at a garden.

Of course there are rules to the form of a *shicchu*. A *shicchu* should be square, four *ken* long on every side,

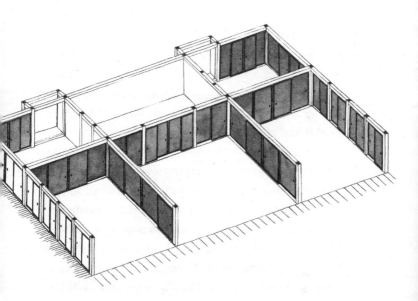

Fusuma painting surfaces in an abbot's residence

open to the garden on the south, and lined with *fusuma* to the east, west, and north. This is exactly what you see at Ryoanji, if you were to look away from the famous rock garden and into the hall—which no one ever does.

On the east-west sides of a *shicchu* chamber, they would use four wide *fusuma*; at the back to the north, eight narrow *fusuma*. This arrangement came to sixteen *fusuma* covering twelve *ken* in total. They also painted on the reverse of the four wide *fusuma* on the east-west sides, so adding that, the total painted area comes to twenty *ken*. The surface area of one *ken*'s width of *fusuma* amounts to 3.476 square meters. So this set of *fusuma* comes to nearly 70 square meters.

But no *shicchu* stands alone. It always has wings, and rooms to the north. The *fusuma* in these adjoining rooms, also painted on the reverse, add thirty-six *ken* more of paintable space. All this adds up to about 195 square meters of painting surface for just one Zen hall!

To give a sense of scale, this is about half the size of the surfaces painted by Michelangelo at the Sistine Chapel, a massive undertaking that took him four years to complete.

Paintings Expand to Fill the Void

An unexpected result of this is that Japan, which we think of as the land of the miniature, actually created one of the larger formats of painting in the premodern world. A Chinese painting master had to cram all his mountains, clouds, and waterfalls into one little hanging scroll; but the Japanese artist had acres of *fusuma* space at his command.

Filling these vast spaces was altogether different from painting a scroll. A hanging scroll called for compression, *fusuma* for expansion. So Japanese artists came up with expansive solutions. Created for *fusuma*, these were also perfect for the grand format of folding screens. New ways of painting came to be.

One way to fill all that space was to paint "Sets." The idea had a long history in China, the standard being "Spring, Summer, Fall, and Winter." Another was "The Four Elegant Amusements," which showed sages or immortals enjoying *koto* or zither, the game of *Go*, calligraphy, and painting. Other variations were "The Eight Immortals," "The Seven Sages of the Bamboo Grove," and "Dragons and Tigers," and so forth.

In China, Sets like these usually consisted of a group of separate paintings. You would sometimes see sets of two, four, or eight scrolls hanging in a Chinese literati's studio.

In Japan, with a room of *fusuma* or a pair of folding screens at his disposal, the painter had the luxury of painting the whole set on one wide canvas. There was space not only for each "Elegant Amusement," but for trees, mountains, rivers, palaces, and lots of gold clouds. The artist had room to play.

So far, with Sets, the Japanese were doing what the Chinese had always done, except larger. But then they tried other techniques. Another way to fill up *fusuma*

"Plum Tree" (Kano school)

Screen of the "Four Amusements"
Right to left: Zither, *Go*, Painting, Calligraphy

254

Top: "Pines at the Beach" (Kano school)
Bottom: "Narcissus" hand scroll by Zhao Mengjian (mid-13th century)

255

space is "Repetition," covering contiguous doors with a lot of just one thing, such as wide stretches of just bamboo. This approach has a hypnotic appeal. It's a form of abstraction.

One subtemple of Daitokuji that I used to frequent had a main hall done only with ink-painted bamboo in this manner. Simple, broad brushstrokes in gray wash rose vertically on *fusuma* bounding three sides of the room—going on and on—bamboo and more bamboo. You could do the same with autumn grasses, pine trees by the beach, flowering peonies or chrysanthemums, or almost any other natural subject.

Like everything else, Japanese artists didn't invent the idea. There's a celebrated hand scroll by the Song dynasty painter Zhao Mengjian called "Narcissus" (a fancy word for daffodils), which is exactly that, narcissus and nothing else. Almost four meters of narcissus leaves and flowers fluttering in the wind. Run your eyes slowly over the repeated lines of long bending leaves and it almost puts you into trance.

"Repetition" in painting is one of those many things the Chinese thought up, dabbled in for a while, then forgot about. But across the channel in Japan, the genre became a huge part of culture. Wonderful as Zhao Mengjian's "Narcissus" scroll is, it never led to much in China. Maybe the idea of repetition of a lot of bamboo or grasses was just too "empty" an idea for the intellectual approach of the Chinese literati. Or perhaps it was the format. Zhao Mengjian's scroll is a psychedelic daffodil experience, much better than real flowers. However, since the scroll's height is only thirty-three centimeters, you have to get up pretty close to it to see anything, and then you have to sit there unrolling it foot by foot before the full effect can sink in.

It takes an effort to look at a hand scroll. Not so for *fusuma*; they come to you. Blown up to the size of sliding doors or folding screens, repeated images make a powerful impact. One such painting that comes to mind is Kano Sanraku's "Peonies" at Daikakuji. It's just peonies and rocks, extending over eighteen gold-leafed doors.

In late Muromachi, painters came up with another way to handle those broad *fusuma* spaces. It's the most adventurous technique of all, which I call "The Slash." It's a purely Japanese solution—I know of no Chinese prototype. One could think of it as a sort of samurai sword slash. Using the approach of "The Slash," artists would take a single plum tree, or a pine, or even one limb of a tree blown up to dramatic proportions, and then paint it in a big diagonal, slashing across a whole wall of *fusuma*.

"The Slash" was a real breakthrough, because with it the painter became, at one stroke, master of the whole huge space that he was painting on.

You can still find numerous examples of "The Slash" in Kyoto—or museums exhibiting paintings that once were in Kyoto. One of the all-time greatest *fusuma* masterpieces is Kano Sansetsu's "Old Plum," which used to be in Myoshinji's Tensho-in subtemple. A massive limb twists and turns, leaping across the surface. It's more of a dragon than a tree. (See page 294)

"Sets," "Repetition," and "The Slash"—none of these are found much in the eras before Muromachi. We're so used to seeing these genres and techniques that we think of them as somehow growing naturally out of an inherent Japanese sensibility. If so, why didn't Japanese paint like that in Heian or Kamakura? There could be no strong and daring Japanese painting before there were *fusuma*.

This is not something that I've ever heard uttered by an art specialist or written in any art book. It's a "Freakonomics"-type twist on the story of Japanese painting, to suggest that sheer square footage could transform the history of art. But it seems that big spaces came first, and sensibility came later.

Once they had learned these techniques, Japanese artists took to them with a vengeance. They applied them to ever-smaller formats, so that what started out large ended up very small, as a slash pattern on gold lacquer, or as a set of woodblock prints.

Extravagant Tokonoma

It didn't stop with *fusuma*. Nowadays most *tokonoma* have plain plaster walls. But in the early stages of *shoin* they covered *tokonoma* walls with paper and painted these surfaces to match the *fusuma* around them. Basically every square inch of a Momoyama room got painted.

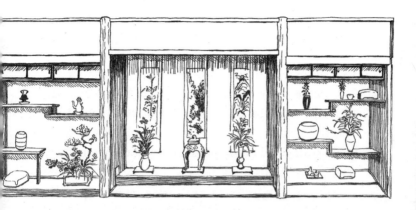

16th century *kazari*

Minimalist Tea-influenced *tokonoma*

They even decorated the back wall of *shoin* display areas that were fitted with staggered shelves. The *tokonoma* painting was the climax in a room of painted *fusuma*, rather like the high note in a soprano's aria. That was the style of Momoyama and early Edo, and you can see it at Nijo Castle, or in the Shiro-shoin hall of Nishi-Honganji, a room that reputedly was modeled after Hideyoshi's Fushimi Castle.

In the painted *tokonoma* they would hang painted scrolls. It was part of the tradition of *kazari* or "decoration." *Kazari* was inspired by the Chinese literati's art collections and love of display. In Japan, they modified this to fit the space and style of *tokonoma* and *shoin*. And of course there were rules. There were *kazari* manuals that showed you just how to arrange flowers, bronzes, incense burners, and so forth.

The thing that doesn't fit today with our idea of "Japanese simplicity" is the over-the-top gorgeousness of it all. They hung paintings on top of paintings. And not just one scroll, but three in a row. And lined up in front of these, crane-shaped bronze candle stands, turtle-shaped incense burners, hand scrolls, and flower vases. These were very busy *tokonoma*.

Romance of the Mud

In the late 15th century, Tea ceremony arrived on the scene, and soon painted *tokonoma* were out. Reacting against the colorful chaos of *kazari* decoration, tea masters pioneered a new spirit of minimalism. They wanted one location in a home or temple with no distractions, where they could place a perfect flower arrangement and hang one precious scroll that would be taken seriously. They carved out the *tokonoma* as their corner of minimalism.

Instead of paper or gold leaf, they preferred a splotchy mud wall, or if they couldn't get that, then at least plain plaster. They favored walls made of clay dug up from the grounds where Hideyoshi's Jurakudai Castle had stood. Called *juraku-kabe* (Juraku plaster), it has a smooth off-white or yellowish texture accented sometimes with rust-like blemishes. Tea masters found it much to their liking, and what began in the tearoom spread to architecture in general.

Today you find *juraku-kabe* used as a standard construction item everywhere in Japan. Modern *juraku-kabe* is a type of mass-manufactured drywall, covered with a plaster-like coating. It should have a little sandy roughness in order to look authentic. You can get it in a range of colors, including shades of blue, green, orange, and pink. It's ironic that the name of Hideyoshi's shining Jurakudai Castle is applied to this bland plaster, since one can be sure that there was hardly a clay surface to be found in the original citadel. Jesuit visitors of the time commented that even the kitchens were gilded. There were no *juraku-kabe* in Jurakudai. It's one of those things that has changed in time and ended up meaning the opposite of what it started out as. The golden palace lives on as the name of a kind of mud.

By mid-Edo, we hardly find a painted *tokonoma*. One of the last really good ones is the grapevine-themed *tokonoma* painted for the abbot's residence of Kinkakuji by eccentric artist Ito Jakuchu at the end of the 18th century. Its grapevines spread riotously, running up to the ceiling, over the *shoin*, and across to the adjacent *fusuma*.

Wooden Doors

After the 18th century, the sober-minded spirit of Tea ceremony took over the *tokonoma* once and for all. There were to be no more vines, sages, waterfalls, and gold leaf in the *tokonoma*. Just sandy plaster, as dull as possible, better to show off hanging scrolls. But colorful *kazari* continued to influence the rest of the interiors of upper-class houses and temples. They still had acres of *fusuma* to paint over. And when they ran out of *fusuma* space, they took to painting on wooden doors.

Doors, made of *sugi* (cedar) boards, had always been there. They survived from old farmhouses. In the old days paper was a luxury, and farmers couldn't afford *shoji* and *fusuma*, so they used wooden doors instead. In Kyoto, a fine wood door made of one large slice of *sugi* can sometimes be seen at the entrance to a corridor. It's called a *mairado*. For an artist, this was a new opportunity, like being given a big canvas of wood grain instead of paper.

Pigments take to wood grain in a special way, so some of these doors are quite striking. If you're looking for fine paintings in Kyoto, you'll find them not only as hanging scrolls and *fusuma*, but also as *mairado*. My favorite *mairado* are a pair of doors with paintings of carp at Shugaku-in Detached Palace. We see the carp through golden nets that cover the entire surface of the doors. Strings of the nets are torn here and there, just as real nets would be. The artist was Maruyama Okyo, a mid-Edo artist who brought Western-style realism into Japanese painting. More precisely, the artist of the nets was Okyo. He added them to a painting of carp done earlier by another artist, for the reason, legend has it, that the carp were escaping every night to swim in the pond in the garden. So the nets are even more realistic than we had imagined.

―――――――

Emptiness

When I said earlier that Muromachi artists painted "every square inch," I meant that there was a painting on every wall. Not that they covered every inch with pigment, as you see in Western oils or frescoes. Within the *fusuma* paintings, there was lots of empty space. Artists call this space *yohaku* (extra white or remaining white) and it's the real secret of those paintings. The painted images float in a great cloud of *yohaku*. Although the word *haku* means "white," the emptiness could also be gold. Easily ninety percent of many so-called "paintings" are *yohaku*, expanses of gold or white on which images stand out like trees against the sky, or rocks in a sand garden.

Yohaku accounts for why, despite the richness of painted surface, old rooms in Kyoto feel light and airy.

When I think about it, the term *yohaku* is really a misnomer, because it implies that the painting is the main thing and the "extra white" is what's left over. Of course that's what we would normally assume. But actually the empty expanse of white or gold is the starting point, and the painting has been supplied as a bit of added decoration. We should call this *yo-e* or "extra painting."

———

Outside Becomes Inside

Now something else comes into play, namely the wooden frames around sliding doors. When we look at the broad expanse of a multi-panel *fusuma* painting, it appears to our eyes as one continuous image, but that's because our minds "edit out" the black-lacquered strips of wood on the edges of the *fusuma*. It's like the way the audience ignores the black-costumed *kuroko* (stagehands) in the Kabuki theater. In fact, the painting is cut clearly into four parts by strong black lines. With folding screens these strips of wood are gone, but you can still see a line between each panel, the hinge where it links to the next panel.

In a Japanese house, when you view the garden, again it appears to your eyes as one wide-open vista. But in reality, wooden pillars at regular intervals break up the view. In other words, whether you're admiring a *fusuma* painting, or enjoying your garden, your view is sliced into sections by vertical lines. People simply got used to that. Views didn't come unbroken, but in segments.

The garden of Entsuji evokes this feeling very strongly, with the view of distant Mount Hiei framed by tall cedar trunks—and at the same time, segmented yet again by the pillars of the room from which one views the garden.

Because of the wide expanses involved in a landscape on *fusuma* or on a screen, you could look at a painting, and feel as if you were gazing out over mountains, gardens, grasses, and willows.

But, of course, if you sat in a room and looked outwards at that very view, sliced into frames by regular pillars, you might also begin to feel that you were looking at a screen.

So it came to pass that the way the Japanese created their gardens was as frontal views that are seen as flat pictures. Treating the garden like a screen and compressing its three dimensions into two gave rise to the idea of *shakkei*, so-called borrowed scenery, where in addition to the foreground—the garden itself with its stones and sand, plants and moss—you would bring a distant view—a mountain or forest or waterfall—into the scene.

Being nearly identical, the flattened segmented space of gardens, screens, and *fusuma* began talking to each other. An effect that worked well in gardens would be adapted for screen paintings, and vice versa.

For example, let's think about all that sand in Kyoto's Zen gardens. There are many theories as to why white sand took over during Muromachi and became the preferred look. You hear much about Shinto and symbolic water and so forth, and I'm sure these played a role. But without getting bogged down in a lot of history and

Top: Entsuji garden

Bottom: Ink landscape on
four-panel *fusuma*

266

symbolism, one could say what the sand does is pretty basic. It's white and it's light. And since way, way, back in time, those two qualities have meant "luxurious" and "noble."

When I look at these dry landscape gardens, I can't help but feel that the white sand is the equivalent of white paper. The black rocks are "painted," as if in black ink, on that surface. Using sand allowed gardeners to spread a big sheet of white paper over a courtyard, and then to use rocks and moss to brush a *sumie* ink landscape on a broad scale.

On the *fusuma*—white paper with black ink mountains, divided by lacquer frames into segments. In the garden—white sand with black stones, this view also divided by wooden pillars into segments. They're mirror images. Eventually the sand moved indoors when they plastered sandy *juraku-kabe* on the walls that weren't paper. There was sand and whiteness everywhere. At night you could hardly tell indoors from out.

———

Dance of the *Fusuma*

In Iya Valley in Shikoku, not far from my thatched farmhouse, is a small old country theater. You can go there and see a thrilling melodrama performed in five acts. However, since this was very remote countryside, getting actors to come and perform was nearly impossible. So there are no actors. The show consists entirely of painted *fusuma*. Not only do these doors slide in their grooves as you'd normally expect, but they rotate from front to back, flip over from top to bottom, they rise up on strings, and in the grand finale, they revolve and realign in a receding perspective, creating the illusion of a vast hall stretching into the distance.

Each turn of the *fusuma* reveals a surprising new vista of painted surface. This form of dramatic art is called *fusuma karakuri* (*fusuma* mechanics). While *fusuma karakuri* belong to hamlets in high mountains, you can see a less complicated version of it on the Kabuki stage at Kyoto's Minamiza theater, when they make a fast set change by sliding *fusuma* while revolving the stage.

Fusuma karakuri seems the final destination of the long process of engineering doors that started way back in the Nara period. From the beginning the Japanese did things with doors that people in other places never did. First they made lattices that hinged up and down; then in Heian they cut the grooves that allowed doors to slide left and right. They made translucent *shoji*, and then thicker *fusuma*. In Muromachi they started painting on those *fusuma*, and nearly every other interior surface. Distinctions between one room and another, between inside and outside, blurred.

Art copied life, and then life copied art. They spread sand, white as paper, in the gardens; adorned the paper walls with images of sand and rock; and plastered the solid walls that remained with clay that looked like sand. In Kyoto, in the malleable interiors of those houses and temples, sliding doors open and close to reveal glimpses of gardens that look like sliding doors. You could say that the old city of Kyoto was itself one vast *fusuma karakuri* show.

Senmen Byobu
"Floating Fans"
screen

Chapter 8

Screens

屏風

Folding screens raise questions.
Such as: What is the origin of the scattering pattern
you see on fan screens?

espite the magnificence of Kyoto paintings, they're a minor genre today. I don't think I've ever met anybody who came to Kyoto specifically to enjoy paintings, as I've had friends who traveled to Venice to see the Tintorettos. Packaged as blockbuster museum exhibitions, shows of famous painters do draw crowds. But very few people seek out paintings in the temples where they are originally situated.

Paintings are something in the background, something you might notice if instead of looking out at a garden, you happened to look in. Visitors to a temple might be impressed by a particularly big painted dragon such as the one at Tenryuji. Or at Nijo Castle, one has the vague sense as one walks along the corridors that there are masses of painted pine trees and flowers amidst the gold-leafed walls of the audience halls. But Nijo is really about grand rooms and squeaky floors. I think a lot of visitors go away from Kyoto after having visited the standard sights without ever really being aware that paintings are the true glory of the city.

When thinking about the places where paintings are to be found, the first thing that comes to mind is of course the *tokonoma* alcove with its hanging scroll. Then there are *fusuma* sliding doors of temples and palaces. But there is another way to display paintings, and that's the folding screen.

Fusuma and *tokonoma* are quite ordinary things. You find them not only in Kyoto temples, but in pretty much every tatami-matted Japanese interior. Folding screens, on the other hand, are today exotic objects.

Screens once existed everywhere, and it was on screens that Japanese painting reached its great flowering in the Edo period. Yet while *tokonoma* and *fusuma* made it into the modern age, screens did not. People living in small modern houses and apartments have no place for a folding screen. You could live in Tokyo for decades and rarely see one except maybe in a museum. Or in a hotel lobby run by one of those international chains who feel that a screen adds a certain Oriental touch. Nowadays the only city in Japan where you would often come across screens is Kyoto.

Screens Unfolding

One way to think of screens is, what you would have if you lifted *fusuma* out from the runners and transoms in which they sat, and made them portable. If you take a set of *fusuma*, remove the wooden strips along the sides, and connect the panels with paper hinges, you get a *byobu*, a Japanese folding screen.

Yet actually folding screens much predate *fusuma*. They were invented by the Chinese and used for hundreds of years before they finally arrived in Japan in the 8th century. There are screens in the Shoso-in treasury in Nara, and they must have been very highly valued because their names show up at the top of the "List of National Treasures" written in 756.

Screens had been around for a long time, but don't seem to have existed in great numbers until mid-Muromachi, when an explosion of folding screens coincided with the explosion of *fusuma*. By adapting the old folding format that had been around for centuries, paintings of a kind formerly found only on *fusuma* doors were now portable.

A room can really handle only one set of *fusuma*. *Byobu*, on the other hand, are easy to take out, look at for a while, fold up, and put out of sight when not needed. This last feature appealed to wealthy temples and feudal lords, as it allowed them to build collections.

Soon every lord and samurai, every wealthy merchant, every inn and restaurant wanted a screen for their reception rooms—so *byobu* multiplied. During the 265 years of the Edo period they were painted in huge numbers. Maybe it was millions. By the end of Edo, there was hardly a household of any substance in Japan that didn't own a screen, and the wealthier homes boasted dozens.

A *byobu* usually consisted of six panels covering a width of roughly two *ken*, just short of four meters wide. Screens usually came in pairs, echoing the way that *fusuma* painted on the same theme would face each other across a room. A complete pair of screens therefore added up to twelve panels.

Sea and Mountains

As I mentioned earlier, in the case of sand and rock gardens, *sumie* ink painting jumped off of *fusuma* into the garden, and the jumping also went the other way. For example, a standard garden format is to lay out the sand and stones as *Horaisan*, "Isles of the Immortals," in the sea. You can arrange the islands at the edges of the garden, so the empty sand becomes a lake or an inlet. Or you can put the islands in the center, in which case the sand is the great ocean surrounding all.

Screen painters picked up on this, and it became a convention of ink-painted landscape screens: mountains on the verges and the sea in the center. Or vice-versa. Six-panel screens always come in pairs, and sometimes artists painted them cleverly so that if you placed the screens side-by-side, you could have either type of view.

The concept of Isles of the Immortals comes from China, but the Chinese never did much with it. It's because the standard Chinese format was a vertical scroll. Of course they did have horizontal hand scrolls, but these are way too narrow for the sea. Hand scrolls are perfect for rivers, so we find plenty of Chinese hand scrolls that depict a journey up a river such as the Yangtze. Come to think of it, a hand scroll *is* a river. It's a "stream of consciousness," revealing new vistas as you unroll it.

In Japan, in contrast, you don't see many paintings of rivers, but constantly the sea. There weren't many big rivers to speak of. And Japan is itself a group of islands in the sea. But it's also because you only start thinking in terms of an all-surrounding sea if you're painting in a large and spread-out format, like *fusuma* or screens. And if, in your rock gardens, you've been looking at oceans of sand.

―――――――――

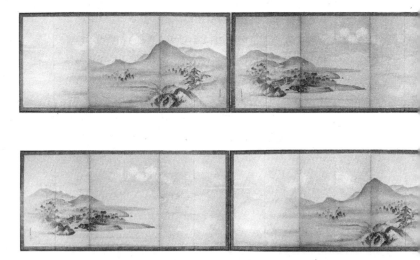

Ink landscape by Kano Eigaku (1790–1867) with left and right screens
in original positions, and reversed

Screens of Many Types

From painting a landscape, screens went on to depict genre scenes such as "Amusements," or "Dancers." For some reason, genre scenes are not something one sees much in *fusuma*. Maybe *fusuma* were inherently too serious. A wall of idle amusements might seem a bit frivolous as the permanent décor for a room. But you could carry a screen into the room, enjoy it, and fold it up again. The "Amusements" screen itself was one of the amusements. *Fusuma* are forever; screens are for fun.

From genre images, they went on to painting the whole city. One type of screen painting is called "Scenes Inside and Outside the Capital" (*Rakuchu Rakugaizu*). These paintings were very detailed, almost like photo albums or maps, because they showed Higashiyama, Yamashina, Uji, and Arashiyama and so forth neatly labeled with little inscriptions on gold paper to tell you where you were.

Screens have come to serve many functions in open-walled Kyoto houses—they divide rooms, lead the way through hallways, or hide things you don't want to show people. Screens can open out wide revealing a misty ink landscape that fills the room; or they can fold up to show just two panels of gold-framed painting, obscuring the tattered *fusuma* that one hasn't gotten around to repairing.

Fusuma had to serve as doors in buildings with standard modules of height and width. But screens could go anywhere and be used for just about anything. So the variations began.

Starting from the basic six-panel *byobu* format, during the Edo period they came up with two-panel, four-panel, and even eight-panel screens. Heights ranged from six *shaku* tall—the *shaku* being the Japanese foot—because that was the height of *fusuma*, down to low three-*shaku* screens called *makura byobu* or "pillow screens." They were handy for putting around *futon* bedding on the floor, kept off drafts, and provided a little privacy.

Like *fusuma*, screens came basically in two formats: white or gold. On the white screens they did *sumie* ink paintings; on the gold they did colors. From this arises the great divide in Japanese painting: "polychrome" and "monochrome" (that is, ink painting).

Ink paintings were considered "high art," so these are very often signed and sealed with the name of the artist. Polychrome painting on gold, on the other hand, was thought of as "craftwork" and often left unsigned, and so we don't have any idea of the painter. We know only that it's "Kano school," or "Tosa school," or some such.

Screens grew to be such a vital part of Kyoto living that people would display their screens publicly during the *Gion Matsuri*. Part of the festival was called the *Byobu Matsuri* or "Screen Festival," where each house would open their frontage to the street and display a prized screen. Many households still do. It was such a colorful and interesting event that artists began to paint screens of the *Byobu Matsuri* during the Gion Festival. So there is a genre of screens that portray houses showing off their screens. Screens of screens.

Painting China

One oddity of classical painting in Kyoto is that you don't usually see Japan. The scene is nearly always China. This is because the Japanese elite viewed China as the locus of high civilization. Just as European painters in France or Italy went on depicting classical Greece and Rome, Japanese artists painted China—an imaginary China none of them had ever seen in real life.

It's been pointed out that the language of the land that gave birth to an art form goes on being the language everyone feels they have to use, long after the art has moved on to other countries. In the early 1600s Italy invented opera, and so most of the librettos written in France and Germany were in Italian right into the late 19th century. Mozart, an Austrian, wrote operas in Italian. When it comes to rock music, the origins lie in England and America, so if you want your rock music to feel authentic, you have to sing in English, whether you're Korean, Swedish, or Icelandic.

In the same way, Japan went on using the visual "language" of China. Screen paintings feature towering peaks of the type that exist in China but not in Japan; immortals and sages in Chinese hats and robes; detailed visions of Hangzhou's "West Lake" or the "Eight Views of Xiao and Xiang Rivers." The Chinese-ness of the art you see in Kyoto is a defining feature, but one that's missed by many visitors. They assume that because they're in Japan, the paintings must be showing Japan.

In fact, almost none of it is. The hairdos held in place by long pins and Confucian caps, loose robes tied with ribbons, flaring rooflines, brick temples and multi-tiered pagodas, spiky mountains, moon windows, and arched stone bridges—all these things proclaim, "This is China."

One of the more curious forms this took was *Noko-no-zu*, "Images of Tilling the Fields," genre paintings that show peasants in the rice paddies; people collecting firewood, making charcoal, spinning silk; and so on. But look closely and you see that these aren't Japanese farmers. The people are wearing Chinese gowns.

In an Imperial nunnery, where a young princess would be sent to dwell in a miniature palace of her own, you will sometimes find a room of *fusuma* painted with images of "Court Ladies Playing with Children." The prettiest version of this is to be found at Reikanji nunnery. The idea was that the princess, living her entire life in a palace and cloister, would not get to play. The *fusuma* were there to show her how much fun it would be to be surrounded by a lot of small children. Given the veneration for all things Chinese, Japanese children would not be considered "elite" enough for a princess. So the children had to be classical Chinese.

The Postage Stamp Problem

Regardless of whether the theme was to be China or Japan, there were different ways to cover the great expanse of paper on a folding screen. You could unify the six panels with one painting that stretched across them all. Or you could paste a series of separate paintings on the panels. A screen like that, called a "mixed

Chinese peasants in an "Agriculture" screen

screen," would consist of twelve paintings of "Immortals," "Hawks," "Birds and Flowers," each framed on its own panel.

That's how the mixing started, but soon people realized that screens could be used as a collage board to mount and display all sorts of things. You could show a collection of small paintings or poetry plaques. I call this the "postage stamp problem." If you collect little things like postage stamps, you'll find it very hard to display them. You can keep them in a box or insert them into folders, but no matter what you do, it involves a bit of trouble to look at them, and in their sheer smallness they don't make a strong impact.

Japanese collectors faced this problem with *shikishi* and *tanzaku* poetry plaques. *Shikishi* (square) and *tanzaku* (rectangular) plaques were pieces of paper only ten to twenty centimeters in size, written in tiny calligraphy by court nobles. They came in sets of thirty-six pieces, "Thirty-Six Sages of Poetry," ten pieces, "The Ten Forms of Poetry," and so forth. As a collector of *shikishi* and *tanzaku*, you could soon end up with hundreds of them.

The problem then was how to display all these little scraps of paper. You could of course mount them in an album, and that was often done. But an album is like a hand scroll—you've got to get up close, hold it in your hand, turn each page, and then you can finally see the pieces. You can never see them all at once. But mount them on a folding screen, and there they are, all spread out before you, enhanced by sheets of gold leaf. These screens are called *shikishi byobu* or "*shikishi* screens."

Scattering

This is where a typical effect of Japanese design came into play. I call it "scattering." Rather than lay out the *shikishi* or *tanzaku* in neat rows and columns, they "scattered" them over the gold-leaf surface, and the spatial effects of this became an art in itself.

Scattering is a minor, even trivial, part of Japanese art that they never mention in art books. *Chirashi*, literally "scattering," is the art of dropping things here and there, seemingly at random—but in a way that's deeply satisfying. It makes no particular sense, but it's perfect. Let's call this "The Art of Satisfying Chaos." It's the manmade version of the chaotic processes of nature, like shorelines and eroded rocks that also give us an unexplainable pleasure. In fact, I've come to believe scattering is really not so minor. It might be the ultimate Japanese thing.

When you start looking for scattering, you find it very early on. In Heian they did it with the meandering cut-and-pasted strips of paper used in the 12th century *Ise-shu* anthology of poetry. In Muromachi *kana* poetry, they scattered calligraphies so thoroughly that you have to jump all over the paper to figure out what comes first and second and third. At Ryoanji's renowned garden, they did it with rocks.

I think this approach to art goes back to primeval, pre-Chinese, original Japanese higgledy-pigglediness. From the beginning in Japan there never was much rhyme or reason; it was *all* scattering. Plenty of symmetry was imported over the centuries from China, but it never quite "took." The default mode was ad hoc, something

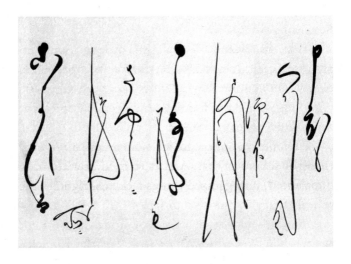

Women's "scattered" calligraphy

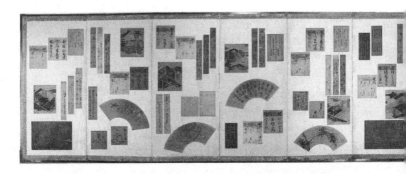

Shikishi screen

here, something there. Why that should be is a deep question, way beyond the scope of our discussion. In any case, people grew skilled at it. If you live by a surfing beach, you get practiced at riding waves. If your surroundings consist of a few buildings over here and a zigzag wall over there, arranged not according to Chinese rules of order, but put together more or less at random, then you adjust to that. Artists learned how to make unbalanced, unorganized things feel "just right"—the appeal of Japanese art in a nutshell.

The skills of scattering had existed all along, but screens took this technique up another notch because of the size of the canvas. Arranging those *shikishi* and *tanzaku* was the ideal training ground for a Mondrian. Once they developed those spatial skills, screen makers moved on to other objects to scatter: small paintings, sections of hand scrolls, fabric cuttings, fans. *Senmen byobu* (fan screens) became a popular style, depicting fans floating down a river or clustering behind a fence.

Finally they ended up with *Tagasode* "Whose Sleeves?" screens on which they painted images of kimono hanging on a rack and blowing in the wind. Sometimes, they pasted pieces from their collections of old textiles for greater effect. These screens hint of an absent lady somewhere outside the picture frame. She would be the "Who."

═══════════

Gold and Silver

In Muromachi and earlier eras, temples and feudal lords favored gold leaf as a painting background, because gold

285

is a chemically "inert" metal. It never tarnishes, like silver does. However, you do see small color variations in old gold leaf due to slight impurities. It might be ninety-nine percent pure gold, but over time that one percent will acquire a faint shade of black or purple.

Instead of using perfectly cut squares as we can do today, gold-leaf artisans applied the leaf in large and small pieces, some nearly square, and others mere fragments. The overlap of these pieces of gold leaf is called *haku-ashi* or "leaf footprints." Where the gold has overlapped, it's stronger in hue; in other places, it's darker. And with the passage of decades or centuries, these changes show up in mysterious and antique patterns.

Looking for *haku-ashi* patterns within the gold leaf of old *fusuma* and screens is one of the pleasures of Kyoto temple spotting. Sometimes these patterns are as exquisite as the paintings. But despite these faint patterns, gold remains basically gold over the centuries. Silver leaf, on the other hand, starts tarnishing immediately, and over months or years ends up black. So silver leaf was avoided.

The literati of mid-Edo discovered the charm of silver. In the tarnished black, you could still see faint traces of silver. Also, on the way from silver to black there were subtle stages, with shades of reflective gray, and hints of orange and bluish-purple. The literati felt that silver had a depth and sophistication that garish gold lacked. And the blue-black tones of tarnished silver went especially well with the black ink of calligraphy.

=====

Bits and Pieces

Sometimes collectors stripped paintings from *fusuma* and remounted them as screens. The telltale sign of this is the round marks where there had originally been metal door-pulls. Paintings that had been mounted on screen panels in sets might get pulled off and remounted one by one as hanging scrolls. Many a scroll you see in *tokonoma* started out this way. It's a fragment of a screen.

And so as time went on, Kyoto paintings got chopped up and put back together into new formats, the bits and pieces tossed into a kaleidoscope of cutting and pasting. *Fusuma* were remounted as screens and screens as *fusuma*, but they might gain or lose a few panels along the way; screens were cut up to become hanging scrolls. Little became big, when *shikishi* and fans were scattered across the surface of one large screen. Big split into small, when they would take a screen fragment, say one bird on a branch, and frame just that.

Calligraphy Screens

Finally, there were "calligraphy screens." With the flowering of literati culture in the Edo period, there grew up a vogue for screens entirely written with calligraphy.

Calligraphy had cachet. Always, both in China and Japan, it had been considered the supreme art of the gentleman, higher than painting. The warrior class preferred calligraphy to paintings because it was pure and abstract. It expressed high ideals found in poems and philosophy. A painting, on the other hand, implied softness and luxury; it could only provide pleasure for an idle aesthete. From the samurai point of view, painting was for wimps.

Calligraphy stirred lofty thoughts in the mind of a stoic warrior. One of the conventions of the Kabuki stage is that the walls of a samurai household will have calligraphy pasted on them; rarely paintings. The kanji on their doors prove that the people of this house dwell on a high moral plane.

Screens made quite an impact on Japanese calligraphy. In China, restricted to narrow hanging scrolls, the standard mode was a pair of scrolls, usually matching couplets. In Japan, however, the calligrapher needed to write a dozen large sheets for a pair of six-panel screens. Once mounted on the screens, the impression created by those big panels, seen all at once, is very strong. Japanese calligraphies, exploding to giant size on screens, developed a power that their Chinese counterparts in the 18th and 19th centuries could never match. The bigger medium became the stronger message.

The Treasure of Kyoto Painting

Well, so far I've talked about the history of how we got *fusuma* and screens, their height, width, surface area, themes, and variations. It reminds me of the explanations of a guide which I heard when I went to see ancient Omiwa shrine south of Nara. People aim their prayers not to an object inside the shrine, the guide explained, but to the whole mountain behind it. He then proceeded to

Calligraphy screen by Ike no Taiga (1723–76)

recite the exact height, weight, and cubic volume of sacred Mount Miwa. I've just done something like this with screens and *fusuma*, and must apologize for all that detail, since the important thing is the paintings themselves.

The treasure of Kyoto wall paintings is so vast as to almost be beyond encompassing. Just to mention a couple of the major pieces, there are the great Kano Eitoku *fusuma* at Juko-in subtemple of Daitokuji; the ink-painted dragons at Gyokuho-in subtemple at Myoshinji; Kano Sanraku's "Plum Tree" *fusuma* at Tenkyu-in, Myoshinji; Hasegawa Tohaku's *fusuma* at Rinka-in, also in Myoshinji. More Tohaku, maybe the greatest of them all, at Chishaku-in. And hundreds of others.

You can go to Beijing and, after hours of tramping through the Forbidden City, hardly come across a painting worth looking at. There must be some in the vaults of the Palace Museum, but very few are on view. What you see is lots of architecture, furniture, and objets d'art. Quite a lot of jade. The only paintings in Beijing that have made an impression on me are the Tibetan *tangka* at Yonghegong, "The Lama Temple," and this is the exception that proves the rule, because they're Tibetan and not Chinese.

I think it's because, with paintings restricted in China mostly to hanging scrolls, where could they hang them? The walls and doors are pierced with fretted windows; rooms are filled with tables, chairs, beds, and lacquer screens. There just isn't as much space for paintings. It could be as simple as that. Meanwhile, in Kyoto, every wall, every door *was* a painting. Even minor temples revel in scores of paintings—some on a grand scale—of incredible finesse and spiritual depth.

Painting in Kyoto reached such a pinnacle because of luck, a "perfect storm" of the right ingredients for genius. First of all, there were lots of displayable space in those empty rooms. There were acres of *fusuma* and screen spaces to be painted. Then, there were wealthy noble families and temples who acted as patrons. There's an old saying that a great family only lasts three generations. But Kyoto nobles and hereditary abbot families survived for a millennium and more. So there was continuity.

To this, add a focus on detailed technique. Extreme care for detail fits in with the obsessive traditional mind-set, and today Japan benefits from that, not only in high-tech industries, but also in high cuisine. That's why *The Michelin Guide* sprinkled its stars so liberally over Japan. Few people in the world are willing to take the meticulous care that Japanese chefs do.

The painters had lots of time to do the honing. The hereditary art studios of the Kano, Unkoku, and Tosa families survived for three to four centuries. You didn't earn the title of "Kano," or "Unkoku," for nothing; you had to apprentice and painstakingly work your way up through a series of ranks.

In the process, the Kanos and Unkokus developed subtle techniques, which the Chinese knew not of. I look at later Chinese painting, and to my Kyoto-centric eyes it looks amateurish. The techniques used in Kyoto had their origin in Ming dynasty China, but the Chinese turned their back on most of them. Well, to give the Chinese credit, looking "amateurish" was part of the value system of the literati. So I guess they got what they were aiming for. Come to think of it, art by Japanese literati could be pretty sketchy, too.

Literati preferred to paint the compact format of hanging scrolls. A few tried their hand at screens and *fusuma*, but basically these belonged to the experts in the Kano, Unkoku, and Tosa schools. In Kyoto they took what they got from the Ming, and built up a huge vocabulary of techniques: how to do ink wash in varying depths and textures; how to draw the line of an old wooden bridge, a cliff with trailing vines, a sage's sleeve, a hint of cloud, fishing nets hanging out to dry, a waterfall fading into mist, a sailboat in the distance, a dragon's whiskers.

For his theme, an artist could elaborate on a story from Chinese literature, or he could be more "Japanese" and narrow the focus down to one simple thing done in hypnotic repetition: peonies, or bamboo, or young pine sprouts. As to who gained a reputation as an artist and who didn't, this is where the eyes of Emperors, shoguns, feudal lords, Zen monks, court nobles, and tea masters came into play.

On top of all this, maybe most remarkable of all, despite five centuries of earthquake, fire, war, and regime change, these paintings on fragile paper and wood are still with us. Miraculous survivors, they're a treasure that rivals the wonders of Florence, Paris, and Rome.

Garden Paintings

Since Kyoto is best known for its gardens, let's take a look at the relation between gardens and paintings. The paintings on the *fusuma* and folding screens—towering peaks, waterfalls hanging in the sky, crooked ancient pines—these were a dream world. Surrealism. Dali, long before we had Dali.

It's very human to want to experience in real life the fantasies that we see painted on our walls—or, popping up on computer screens. The 18th century lords living in the great homes of England had many a painting of romantic Greek and Roman ruins on their walls. Not content just to enjoy them in oil, they went and built faux "ancient ruins" in their gardens. To make the effect more realistic, they even hired "ornamental hermits" to live on the grounds, who had to sign a contract agreeing for a certain length of time never to cut their hair. The lords wanted their ruins to look authentic.

Something similar happened in Kyoto. The standard name for landscape paintings is *sansui*, literally "mountains and water." *Sansui* is a peculiar word in that, if you just think of the meaning of the kanji that make it up (山水), "mountains and water," it could naturally have been used for real-life "landscape." In fact, the dictionary defines *sansui* as "landscape." But people never use it that way. When you see the word, it typically refers to a painting, not actual mountains and rivers. The term we use for sand gardens is *kare-sansui* or "dry landscape," which orients it to painting by its very name.

So the true translation of *kare-sansui* should be not "dry landscape," but "dry landscape painting." In Kyoto's gardens they scrupulously reproduced all the conventions of *sansui* ink painting. They pruned branches so they would look like they had been brushed in black ink. They arranged rocks to look like islands in a painted sea. For added authenticity, in the place of painted sages, they had real-life Zen monks to rake the gravel.

We know from old records that the garden at Ginkakuji was designed to be a miniature of China's Dongting Lake and the Xiao and Xiang rivers. Of course, that garden was not modeled after the real lake or rivers, which no Japanese had ever seen. It's a copy of *paintings* of those places. The shogun commissioned Kano Masanobu to paint scenes of Xiao and Xiang on the *fusuma* of his palace (now disappeared). For added emphasis, he had his favorite calligraphers write Xiao and Xiang poems, which were pasted on top of the paintings. So the temple had Xiao and Xiang images painted on the walls inside, sculpted in sand and rocks in the garden outside, with poems to prove it.

Of the gardens of Kyoto, the one at Juko-in at Daitokuji well evokes—in the medium of sand and stones—the world of ink painting that one would usually see on doors or screens. Sen no Rikyu created it based on a draft brushed by painter Kano Eitoku, who also did the *fusuma* in the hall facing the garden. The foreground of Rikyu's garden is just flat earth, maybe once just sand, now mostly moss. It's the flat, unpainted, lower surface of a screen. In the back runs a row of rocks, some higher, some lower, a range of distant painted peaks. In the middle of these rocks lies a flat stone—the *de rigueur* bridge that appears in mountain paintings. It's a dream landscape by Eitoku, executed in stone instead of ink.

Read the many books on gardens, and you find that the experts expend much effort trying to understand the spatial relationships between rocks. What hidden rules guided the gardeners when they put this rock here and not there? I think it becomes less mysterious when we think of gardens as two-dimensional paintings that expanded into three. There were rules, but they're the "flatland" rules of classical ink painting.

The gardens of Kyoto were attempts to take the fantasyland of painting and re-create it in the physical world, using real-life materials like gravel, stone, moss, trees—and monks. As such I must confess to a twinge of disappointment sometimes when I see one of these gardens. They're just too "real." Yes, that's a lovely old pine tree pruned into a picturesque pose. But could one branch of this real tree outgrow its parent, like a mighty branch in a *fusuma* painting, and twisting at shocking angles as it goes, leap across twenty feet of gold? That stretch of sand is quiet and meditative. But could it compare with the atmospheric nothingness of the "Dawn Landscape," just hinted at with a few streaks of watery ink, on the white-papered wall in the back room at Shinju-an?

Eitoku, when he saw Rikyu's garden at Juko-in, must

Top: "Plum Tree" by Kano Sanraku at
Tenkyu-in, Myoshinji

Bottom: Kano Sansetsu's "Old Plum"
formerly in Tensho-in, Myoshinji

have felt a smile come to his lips, because he knew that Rikyu's row of drab little rocks lined up against a garden wall could never compare with what Eitoku could achieve with a few bold ink strokes.

Gardens are the movie version of the book. We may have loved the movie, but the book is usually better. It's because imagination will always trump reality. I think that's why garden-making never ranked as a "high art" in Kyoto. The best ones were created by monks in their spare time such as Muso Soseki, or tea masters such as Murata Juko and Sen no Rikyu, who are better known for other things. We have no record of who designed most of the others, even the supreme garden of them all, Ryoanji, whose authorship is a complete mystery.

We do know the name of Shogun Ashikaga Yoshimasa's favorite gardener, whose son is credited with the garden in Ginkakuji. He was Kawaramono Zen'ami, and from his name we can glean what the status of a gardener was in those days. *Kawaramono*, "a person from the riverbed," was a term used for the poorest of the poor, beggars and homeless. The Kamogawa riverbed was where outcasts lived. Criminals were beheaded there. In later years, Kabuki was born on makeshift stages along the riverbed. Forever after, Kabuki actors bore the stigma of being called *kawara-kojiki* or "beggars from the riverbed," and in Edo days it was a crime for them to consort with samurai.

Zen'ami and his descendants, and other gardeners like them were known as *sansui-kawaramono* or "landscape beggars." In short, a gardener, unless he happened to be a monk, ranked with outcasts. In contrast, the artists who painted Kyoto's *fusuma* and screens, such as Hasegawa Tohaku, Kano Tan'yu, and later, Ito Jakuchu, were superstars, celebrated as incomparable masters in their own time.

═══════════

Modern Paintings and Copies

As important as painting was to Kyoto culture, in modern times it has become rather hard to enjoy it. Many of the great works are locked away in subtemples of big establishments such as Daitokuji or Myoshinji, which keep their gates tightly closed except for rare public viewings. You've got to keep your eye out for when these paintings are going to be shown to the public, and then arrange to visit them during the brief window that they're open. They don't allow you to photograph the paintings at most temples, nor do they usually sell illustrated books or pamphlets about them. Even postcards are hard to find. It's all wrapped in deep secrecy.

My library shelves sag under the weight of dozens of volumes on the gardens of Kyoto. So far, I haven't been able to find even one book on the paintings of Kyoto. So it's natural enough that visitors end up not looking at paintings. However, when I think of the moments when I held my breath in awe, when I was truly stirred and stood there stock still in amazement, it's when I first caught sight of one of these masterpieces.

Well! We've got off onto a vein of gushing admiration,

the usual tone of the stuff that people write about Kyoto. It's really not my style. What could have gotten into me? It's time, then, to grumble a bit and point out the downside. Before we conclude this chapter, I need to add that there are plenty of really bad wall paintings in Kyoto.

If you were to rank them, the worst would be where they've removed the originals to preserve them, and put cheap copies in their place. In fact, copies are becoming the rule rather than the exception. When you're standing in front of the famous *fusuma* at a great temple, you're very likely looking at facsimiles. There's a good reason for this, namely the fragility of paper. Exposed to too much light, paper "burns" just like our skin sunburns. For centuries the paintings survived in relatively good condition because of the darkness that Tanizaki praised so highly. Two or three times yearly a temple would open up its hall for a ceremony. The rest of the time, the paintings slept in the semi-darkness of dim light seeping through *shoji* from the garden.

Along came the 20th century, and the crowds and the light burst in. Paintings began to degrade. You can see sunlight damage at many temples where the paper has browned, or large bits have flaked off. Over time, sunlight is as big an enemy as war and fire. The only ways to preserve the paintings for posterity are either to limit the number of visitors who can see them (which is one reason why many temples open so rarely), or to make copies.

Copies are unavoidable, and not necessarily such a bad thing. With modern technology, originals can now be duplicated so well that even an expert eye could hardly see the difference. So I wonder why there are so many really poor copies around Kyoto. The main hall of Nijo Castle is one of the saddest examples, with copies in plasticky blue and hospital-wall green that bear hardly any resemblance to what was once there. If you want to get a sense of what those paintings really should be, take a look at some originals still at Nijo Castle, which they haven't yet gotten around to replacing. They're in the smaller halls that you pass through on the way to the main room. The paints, brilliant yet subtly graded, were made from crushed minerals such as cinnabar and malachite. The gold leaf has aged over centuries to reveal intricate *haku-ashi* patterns. Given the fact that they have the technology to do so much better, it's baffling why Nijo went this way. I suppose it's the "final destination" of anything controlled by bureaucrats.

On the other hand, at Chishaku-in temple, they've installed in the main hall a stunningly garish copy of their famed Hasegawa Tohaku *fusuma*. So I guess we can't blame this on bureaucrats alone.

One rung up from this are the newly painted *fusuma* of the last forty or fifty years. One might mention the cartoonish gold lotuses on the modern *fusuma* at Shoren-in. While they may be a bit jarring at first sight, they have a light almost *kawaii* feel to them. In general, what you'll notice about many of the newer paintings is that they've given into the temptation to cover every square inch with color. They're strong, insistent statements. The mysterious empty spaces (*yohaku* "extra white") in which the old paintings floated have disappeared.

Deep Kyoto

The appeal of what is sometimes called "Deep Kyoto" lies in the fact that it's still alive. In this it stands in marked contrast with Beijing, which overflows with treasure ten times greater in scale than Kyoto, but it's all just "relics." The Forbidden City and Temple of Heaven, with the Emperor long vanished, function as tourism mills managed by party committees. Temples with no believers; traditional arts that exist only to supply tourist trinkets. In Kyoto, practicing monks and priests run the hundreds of religious establishments, large and small; millions of Japanese still believe deeply in their religious principles. Headquarters of Tea ceremony, Noh drama, flowers, and so forth have found modern relevance.

When we look at what survived from the past and thrives today in Kyoto, we can see that ceramics, garden and teahouse design, and traditional crafts such as weaving, bronze and silver casting, and bamboo work not only made it into the 21st century, but each has given birth to modern masters of world-level importance.

In garden design, Shigemori Mirei created gardens from the 1930s to the 1970s that are among Kyoto's most popular. At an artistic level they vie with Muromachi masterpieces. In pottery, the city boasts many distinguished artists. But painting has struggled. Of course the temples, being still alive, continue to have a demand for new art works. There are plenty of rooms that need *fusuma* and screens painted. Unfortunately, the artists commissioned for those paintings have mostly been non-entities.

Of the modern *fusuma* painters, Domoto Insho is the most important. Insho, who died in 1975, was a Kyoto-based "modernist in Japanese style" who became the most favored *fusuma* painter for temples. I think you could read many a guidebook, and while Insho's name might crop up, he would hardly be given major treatment. When you actually come to Kyoto, however, like it or not you'll see more of him than any other artist. Insho's work adorns *fusuma* at Toji, Honen-in, Saihoji, Ninnaji, Chishaku-in, Tofukuji—all over the city in fact, not to mention at the Insho-Domoto Museum close to Kinkakuji. You may never get to see a real Tan'yu or a Jakuchu, but you'll be sure to see plenty of Insho. He thrived in 20th century Kyoto because he fulfilled temples' need to look suitably modern.

Shigemori's gardens just get better with time. Not so with the modern *fusuma* paintings. Mostly Insho and his fellow "modernists in Japanese style" have not aged well, and more recent painters have had even less success. One wishes that modern-day temples had heeded that old book of court ritual that said, "All the *fusuma* should be white."

You always hear about how in Japanese houses the *tokonoma* is where the art is. But if you look at the temples and palaces of Kyoto, as well as old houses, the art is on walls and along corridors; it's on *fusuma* doors and on gold screens. The *tokonoma* is just an afterthought.

Senbon Enma-do
Left to right:
The Recorder, Enma Dai-o,
the Announcer of the Verdict

Chapter 9

閻
魔
堂

Enma-do

In Kyoto the afterlife is not far away:
the Door to the Underworld, the Guide of Souls,
and the King of Hell are all here.

I sometimes think about the differences between modern art and traditional art. I ask myself why I feel such a passion for antiques and old forms of music or dance. When modern art or performance does interest me, it usually draws in some way from the wellspring of tradition.

Clearly, modern art that's transcended all the stodgy old limits and conventions has the upper hand. It reflects our time and reveals what's possible with new technologies. That said, and while knowing I should take more interest in contemporary art, I find that I still prefer old things.

Kabuki actor Tamasaburo once said that a characteristic common to all classical performing arts is that *they take time*. I think Tamasaburo has said something important there, because the appeal of old things does seem to have something to do with the time that people once had at their disposal, the time it took to create something, the time that people had to think about these things in the old days.

A Tibetan adept would go into a cave and meditate for decades until the form of a particular goddess appeared and he could see with his own eyes the flashing details of her rolling heads and spinning hands, each one brandishing a device that symbolized and emitted yet other manifestations. In Japan, in the Heian, Kamakura, and Muromachi periods, people had a lifetime to meditate on and think about the concepts expressed in religious painting. What is "Compassion," what is "Wisdom," what is "Death," who is the "Guide of Souls"? The carvers of religious sculpture were often monks who dedicated their lives to religious practice. There was time put into these things.

Another critical aspect about traditional art is that it came out of the *human heart*. It's the heart versus the mind.

In earlier times we didn't know about science or logic, nor the discoveries and thinking processes that went into modern enlightenment. I'm not talking here about nostalgia for an ancient era because I can tell you that when I have a toothache, I am very glad that I'm not living in the 18th century. Nevertheless, because the art works of the premodern era came out of the heart, out of natural rhythms, at a remove from what we now know scientifically about the universe, they were free to fly far out beyond the limits of "reality." They can be (to our modern eyes) wildly illogical and fantastical. Beyond the pale.

Weird and Wonderful

Classical Esoteric Buddhist art with its many-headed, multi-armed deities surrounded by flames, clouds, and mythical animals verges on being plain whacky, with some truly bizarre formulations. One might ponder for a minute on the finest collection of statues in Kyoto—perhaps the single most important intact group of old wooden sculptures in the world—the Buddhas and guardian figures of Sanjusangendo (The Hall of 1001 Buddhas). Sanjusangendo miraculously survived a hundred fires and earthquakes since it was built in the late 12th and early 13th century.

The hall contains one large statue of Kannon, "God of Compassion," in the center, with five hundred smaller Kannons arrayed in ten rows on rising plinths on each side. The Kannons are sculpted in the smooth, impassive style of late Heian. Elegant they are, but their multi-armed bodies are about as far from human as a collection of a thousand spiders.

In front of these stand twenty-eight super-realistic pieces done in Kamakura style. They posture and bluster with animated force starkly in contrast with the Heian stillness. A fierce wind (what I call the "Kamakura gale") gusts through them, waving draperies and ribbons, while smoke and flames whirl over their heads. Each statue features some outré twist of the imagination: a god with a beaked garuda-bird head playing a flute; foreheads sporting three eyes or five eyes; a warrior grappling a dragon; and other guardian figures poised like body-builders to show off their rippling musculature—where people don't have muscles. Like the gargoyles on European cathedrals, it's medieval grotesquerie. Such was the weird and wonderful world of Esoteric Buddhism.

The strangeness and whimsy are difficult for modern people to accept. The plethora of gods and magic powers feels like "superstition," which is old-fashioned and embarrassing, and anyway, trying to learn the meaning of it all takes too much *time*. So foreigners drawn to Buddhism in Japan usually prefer to bypass all that Esoteric extravaganza, and go for Zen minimalism.

Horse-Headed Kannon, Joruriji temple

The Dreamtime

On the surface, Zen is the easy way out. You can have a quiet meditation overlooking a bit of raked sand—an escape from the disturbing nightmarish visions of ancient Hinduism and Esoteric Buddhism. Think of the so-called "Horse-Headed Kannon" statue found in old Esoteric temples in the Kyoto-Nara area. What is that? Why should the "God of Compassion" have a horse's head? This is imagery from a dream world. The Australian aborigines called it "Dreamtime." But of course, dreamtime is not unique to the Australian aborigines. I think it was something that all humans shared until the coming of the modern age. The dreamtime was expressed in traditional arts, and that is part of the inexplicable appeal of old things.

The dreamtime exists even in Zen, for Zen too comes to us from an old time. Those who feel that they've found in Zen a pure escape from bizarre old superstitions are deluding themselves. The Zen "look" as we find it in gardens may seem simple enough, but Zen literature and calligraphy, with their zany humor and mocking paradoxes, are as weird as anything the ancient Hindus ever dreamed up.

Zen has its own taste for the outlandish, fueled by the ideal of a Zen adept, living on a plane beyond the conventionalities of normal people. From Muromachi onwards, Zen ink painting lovingly depicts its sages and patriarchs in playful and enigmatic scenes: an immortal dangling a crab, Bodhidharma crossing the Yangtze while standing on a reed, or the Tang poet-monks Kanzan and Jittoku laughing at an empty scroll. You see paintings like this all over Kyoto, each one a joke with a Zen punch line.

I remember years ago seeing the abbot of one of the Zen temples, while giving a talk to some visitors, suddenly jump into the flawless sand garden, leaving everyone gaping in astonishment. It was a painting of Zen eccentricity come to life.

In the 17th century, the taste for eccentricity reached its height in a vogue for statues and paintings of *rakan*, "perfected beings," known as *arhat* in Sanskrit. Rows of *rakan* sit in the upper stories of the larger temple gates, gesticulating in the gloom as crowds walk below. There's a striking group of the "Eighteen *Rakan*" arrayed on either side of the Daiyuhoden hall in Manpukuji in Uji. Manpukuji, head temple of the Zen Obaku sect, was founded by the Chinese Zen master Ingen. The *rakan* of Manpukuji, carved by a sculptor brought over from China, sprout bulbous heads and super-long arms; one holds a bowl in his hand from which rises a dragon head; another pulls open his ribcage to reveal a Buddha inside. This, too, is Zen.

There's a decorous tourist-friendly Kyoto, epitomized by the Philosopher's Walk with its pretty canal lined with cherry trees. You can take a nice stroll here while feeling happily aesthetic. But elsewhere in the city, haunting reminders of the old dreamtime still lurk, pockets of strange things that don't fit into our modern ideas. They float like flotsam and jetsam randomly in downtown

Above and facing: *Rakan*, "perfected beings," Manpukuji

Kyoto, which is now largely an expanse of parking lots
and apartment blocks looking much like any other city of
Japan. But somewhere buried amongst them you fall upon
odd little places that have a twilight zone feeling. You
walk through a gate and suddenly it's goodbye to rhyme

or reason. Zen aesthetics will be no help to you here.

One example of that would be the little temple to Marishiten, a few blocks south of Shijo along Yamato-oji. Marishi, which literally means "light," was seen in ancient India as the Queen of Heaven. During the years of samurai warfare in the 15th century, warriors prayed to Marishi for victory, and from this comes the deity's modern significance, which is that it is the "God of Chance." Marishi is the one you pray to if you want to win the lottery.

Bodhisattvas and protective deities like Marishi often ride an animal that is their "vehicle," such as Monju's lion or Fugen's elephant. In the case of Marishi, it is a team of wild boars. The reason is that wild boars run very quickly; they run at the speed of light. That was the concept—speed. So, here stands this little temple of the "God of Chance," a god riding a team of seven boars running at the speed of light, and all around it stand statues of boars granting good luck to anyone who has to win a bet or a contest. The temple and the boars sit there ignored and largely unknown in a little corner of Higashiyama, just behind Kenninji temple.

———————

The Lord of Hell

I've lived in Kyoto for decades, but it was only recently that I visited the temples to the "Lord of Hell." I read a notice somewhere that the right time to visit them is the August *Obon* festival. I'd wanted to go for a long time and thought that this was my chance. As part of my mid-life crisis, I'd been reflecting on what I was really doing with my life, and it occurred to me that perhaps I should pay a visit to Enma, the Lord of Hell.

After death you are tried and judged at the court of Enma. He's a fearful god related to Yama, the Tibetan

Wild boar statue

"God of the Dead." In fact, Yama and Enma are basically the same word. Enma weighs your actions in this life, and then declares which of the "Six Ways" you will be reborn into, and if your destination happens to be Hell, he decides your special punishment.

It's very bureaucratic because the concept comes via China. The Chinese vision of the afterlife looked very much like their vision of this life, namely bureaucracy. So, on either side of the Lord of Hell sit officials with brushes and scrolls, keeping track and filling out forms in triplicate. On the Lord of Hell's right, his mouth wide open, is the "Announcer of the Verdict." To the left, with his mouth tightly closed and his hand holding a brush, is the "Recorder," who writes it all down as a record for the court.

———

The Cosmic *"Ah"*

The open and closed mouth, known as the rule of *Ah Un*, came up earlier when we were talking about gates. It arises from *Ah* and *Om*, the first and last letters of the Sanskrit alphabet. When it traveled eastward to Japan, it became *Ah Un* and when it went westward it became *Alpha Omega*, which you see carved on either side of a Byzantine altar. It means beginning and end, *Yin* and *Yang*, sound and silence, giving and receiving; and therefore includes the whole world.

In East Asia, *Ah Un* merged with the idea of *mantras*, "holy sounds" that have magical power. Ever since the

Beatles, Indian and Tibetan gurus have popularized *Om* as a sacred syllable, but people don't talk so much about the *Ah* part, although both are of equal importance. If *Om* is the end, then *Ah* is the beginning. In Japan there is an entire school of meditation known as *ajikan meiso*, "meditation on the character for *Ah*," which is a major practice in Esoteric Buddhism.

So, following the rule of *Ah Un*, one of Enma's two officials has his mouth open, and the other's mouth is closed. Enma, meanwhile, bears a furious, enraged expression with his mouth gaping and his eyes bulging. He's wearing a wide black hat, the power-hat of a magician or a judge, with something like a chopstick through it that binds the hat to his hair. At the top of the hat is the character *O* (王), meaning "King," because at the end, "Death" is the king of all; nothing surpasses him. Enma Dai-o (The Great King Enma) is the ultimate king, which we tend to forget in our daily lives. That wide-open mouth of Death is emitting the cosmic "*Ah!*" which supersedes all the other *Ahs* and *Oms* of the universe.

―――――

Burial Grounds

Kyoto's main shrine to Enma, Senbon Enma-do, stands smack at the center of what had been the ancient city. It was built along Suzaku-oji, the central axis in the old geomantic layout of Kyoto. Named after Suzaku the "Vermillion Bird," the god of the cardinal direction of the south, the street ran due south from the Imperial

Palace to Rashomon, the main gate to the city. Over time, the central axis shifted east, eventually settling on Karasuma street where it remains today. As for Suzaku-oji, it lost its role as a major artery and became relatively minor Senbon street.

As a side note, in Japan the typical scenery of a village or town in the countryside features four levels. The highest level is the mountains looming beyond the town—this is where spirits dwell. The medium level, the foothills, is where the temples or shrines are located. At the base of the mountain, we find clusters of houses where people live; and from there, the lowest level, fields and rice paddies spread out into the flat plains.

Kyoto's street grid comes from China, but the spatial flow of mountain-to-foothills-to-plains is native Japanese. Rippling outwards from the Imperial Palace at the center are the streets and avenues along which people live and work; but the horseshoe of mountains to the north, west, and east has always been, as it was in the old days for every village, the realm of gods, demons, and ghosts. Nowadays most of the large temples and shrines are to be found along this horseshoe of hills, protected and off limits to developers. In other words, the spirits still live there.

In Heian, long before the temples that we know today were built, these hills were the burial grounds. There were three: Adashino to the west, Toribeno to the east, and Rendaino to the north. The graveyard in the north was considered the most important since one had to pass along the city's central avenue, Suzaku-oji, to get there, which is why Enma-do was built on this avenue, at the heart of the old city. The "Temple of Death" stood on the way to the graveyard.

As the city center moved to the east, the graveyards to the north and west faded in importance. The northern burial grounds seem to have been largely forgotten. In 1903, Adashino Nenbutsuji, located near what had been the graveyards to the west, collected hundreds of stone Jizo statues from areas around Kyoto, and set them up in an eerie courtyard. All that's left of the memory of the western graveyards is this courtyard of mossy stones. Today, the main burial grounds lie at the eastern edge of the city, notably the Otani graveyards located just south of Kiyomizu temple. The *Gozan Okuribi*, burning of large characters on the mountainsides ringing Kyoto, light the way for returning spirits at *Obon* time. These fires refer back to the fact that the burial grounds were once located in the hills.

The Guide of Souls

While we're on the subject of graveyards and death, the most popular god of the underworld is Jizo Bosatsu, the bodhisattva who is the "Guide of Souls." Jizo protects us after death, especially little children. Images of Jizo show him in the guise of a traveling monk, often with a gentle or even sweet expression, carrying a pilgrim's staff and holding a *hoju*, a bright Dharma Jewel lighting our way through the underworld.

Top left: Jizo, "Guide of Souls"

Top right: Jizo stone with robe
offering

Bottom left: Modern-day Jizo

Bottom right: Jizos in the moss
at Sanzen-in temple

While Jizo's cult is a minor one, he's hugely popular. There are only a few temples devoted to Jizo, but nearly every temple will have a Jizo sculpture in the grounds somewhere. Little statues of him are to be found in the millions throughout Japan, along every sort of passageway, from temple paths to motor highways. These far outnumber all the other bodhisattvas put together.

Over time, the idea of Jizo as the guide of souls developed into the idea of protector of travelers, and in this capacity, he got associated with the phallic stone markers that stood at the crossroads. And so figures of Jizo took the shape of rounded stones. You see them by the roadside, sometimes covered with a little "bib" of colored cloth. Originally, this was an abbreviated version of a gift of Buddhist robes to Jizo, who is always depicted as a shaven-headed monk. Nowadays the bibs are simply a way of offering a prayer, often to do with the health of children. However, the bibs have outgrown Jizo, and even Buddhism. You'll see them offered to all sorts of divinities, including stone lions on either side of temple gates, and fox statues at Fushimi Inari shrine.

Jizo saves children from suffering, and is also the guide of children who have died young, including infants lost before birth. So in modern times, Jizo has come to be depicted as a child. With that as the starting point, in this day of *kawaii* cuteness, you can just imagine what has happened to the image of Jizo. From the sad-faced wooden statues and mossy stones of the past, Jizo has morphed into the ultimate cute manga-bodhisattva. *Kawaii* has entered the underworld, and there can be no turning back.

As with anything, do enough of it and eventually someone will create a masterpiece. In the case of the *kawaii* Jizos, this happened at Sanzen-in temple in Kyoto's far north. Known for its wide expanse of brilliant green moss, Sanzen-in at some point buried some supercute child Jizo statues in the moss. At first people were a little shocked that the *kawaii* cult had been brought right into the heart of a beloved garden with hundreds of years of history. But as time has passed and the moss has grown over the stone Jizos, these cute little things have taken on a real poignancy.

<hr />

Senbon Enma-do

Leaving Jizo aside for a moment and returning to Enma, according to tradition, Senbon Enma-do was built by Ono Takamura, a Heian-period courtier with shamanistic powers. Takamura was medieval Japan's Merlin. He is said to have commuted between the Imperial Palace above ground during the day and Enma's Palace below ground at night. The original temple burned like almost everything else in Kyoto during the Onin War (1467–77) and was rebuilt after that, again and again. The present temple is unassuming, a cluster of small buildings that appear to be only a few decades old. In the garden is a little collection of stone Jizos and some old tomb monuments.

Inside, however, hidden behind lattice windows that only show his terrible eyes, stands the statue of Enma dating back to 1488. The legend is that these are the original amber eyes that were recovered from the fires of the Onin War. Enma's eyes are fierce, and they're also a little bit sad, because Enma, as it turns out, is just another manifestation of Jizo. These angry amber eyes are also the loving eyes that guide us.

Enma and Jizo, angry and sad, are two faces of Death. There are other faces, of course, some demonic, and some even funny. Several times a year, Senbon Enma-do puts on a series of old-style morality plays, known as *Nenbutsu Kyogen*. Along with similar plays performed by masked dancers at Mibudera and Seiryoji, these are known as the "Three Morality Plays of Kyoto." In the others the actors mostly perform in pantomime, but at Senbon Enma-do they speak, and the dialogue is often comic. In one play, for example, a dead soul encounters a demon who starts to torment him. But when they consult Enma's "Recorder," it turns out that the dead soul had been a good man. So the tables are turned, and in the end the demon has to carry the dead soul on his back all the way up to Heaven.

Enma is an avatar of child-loving gentle Jizo, and therefore his image conjures up a mix of qualities: rage, grief, sadness, and even laughter. It is questioning what you've done with your life. I don't think in all my years in Japan I've ever seen a more powerful sculpture than what I saw that day of my visit.

It's not the most refined statue; it's actually a bit coarse, provincial looking. It was built in a rough and tough period, a poor and ravaged age of Japanese history, a time when the city stood largely deserted, nobles had fled to the countryside, and the Imperial family scraped by in poverty within the palace ruins. So this doesn't stand aesthetically at the same level as the finely polished Heian or magnificently modeled Kamakura sculptures at Sanjusangendo. This comes from an interregnum, a murky period that people don't know much about; it's done in a style that we are not familiar with; a thing unto its own.

One thing that I've learned as an art collector is that if there is "only one in the world," you would think it would be incredibly valuable. But it doesn't work that way. The thing of which there is "only one" has no museums collecting it, and no scholars studying it. And therefore it is not necessarily valued. This statue of Enma falls into that category. That may account for why it has never been designated an Important Cultural Property; and you'd hardly find a mention in any history of art, or even most guidebooks.

When looking at Enma I thought of a haiku I read years ago by Buson. The father of my scroll mounter, Kusaka, was a great lover of haiku and poetry. He told me once that I'd better learn some haiku or I wouldn't be literate. So he gave me his worn old haiku book, which I went off and read, and I was struck by one vivid poem by Buson—in fact, I can hardly remember any others from that book:

En-o no	閻王の	King Enma's
kuchi ya botan o	口や牡丹を	mouth. Peonies
hakanto su	吐んとす	about to be spat out.

The bright red peonies suggest the shocking vermillion of Enma's open mouth, but also the resurgent force

The Stripping Crone, Datsueba

of late spring and early summer when peonies bloom. It has, as haiku always must have, a seasonal aspect to it.

———————

The Three Enmas of Kyoto

While I don't know of anyone specializing on the Enma statue at Senbon Enma-do, you could certainly write a thick book on the subject of the cult of Enma in general. Enma used to be everywhere in Japan, and in old towns you'll often find a little Enma-do temple standing at a forgotten corner. For one week during *Obon*, when the departed spirits return to us, many Enma temples display paintings called *Jigoku-e*, "Hell Paintings," displaying in detail the realms of Hell and the gruesome torments that departed spirits must endure: being sawed in half, boiled in vats, and beaten by devils wielding nasty spiked batons.

Hell is of course much more interesting than Heaven, which is why everyone reads Dante's *Inferno*, and nobody reads *Paradiso*. William Gilkey, occultist and my personal guru who lived near me in Kameoka, used to say that none of us can imagine the bliss of Heaven because we've never experienced it. Would it be singing endlessly in angelic choirs? What if you didn't like harp music? But Hell is something we know quite well.

The Chinese, Japanese, Tibetans, Thai, and Balinese all relish Hell paintings. In Kameoka there's a small Enma-do standing insignificantly along the road I take every day to the station. For most of the year it's closed, but around *Obon* they open the doors, and display an eight-foot-high "Hell Painting," covered with hundreds of Hieronymus Bosch–like figures suffering every manner of ghastly punishment. As with a Bosch, it's hard to resist the voyeuristic fun of it all. It's unexpected to find something so ghoulish and colorful lurking just across the street from a big supermarket in the bland suburb that Kameoka has become.

Kyoto has not just one, but several Enmas. Among my favorites is the Enma statue in Rokuharamitsuji temple; an old survivor built near the site of Taira Kiyomori's palace. For connoisseurs of Enma, this one, while smaller than the one at Senbon, is especially fine. It's early, dating to the Kamakura era, and comes complete with a little statue of Datsueba, the fearsome old crone who strips the souls of the dead of their clothing before they cross the stream to the other world.

On the same day that I visited Senbon Enma-do, I also paid respects to Rokudo Chinnoji, another Enma temple at the eastern edge of the city, near Matsubara Higashi-yama. This, too, has ties to the shaman Ono Takamura, and inside there is a statue of Enma and Takamura himself. In Japan, everything comes in threes: "Three Great Gardens," "Three Famous Views," and of course the "Three Morality Plays of Kyoto." In that vein, I would add the sculpture of Enma at Chinnoji to the Enmas at Senbon and Rokuharamitsuji to make up the "Three Enmas of Kyoto."

The Gate to the Underworld Next Door

For decades I've walked past this temple and its big red gate is usually closed, but it was open on that day. There's a stone monolith in front of the red gate which reads: *Rokudo-no-tsuji*, "The Crossroads of the Six Ways."

The Six Ways are the cycles of rebirth, and this concept flourishes not only in Japan, but in Buddhism everywhere. In Tibetan or Mahayana Buddhism all across Asia, from Mongolia down to Vietnam, you see paintings on the theme of a *mandala* of the "Six Ways," into one of which every living thing is to be sent according to its deeds in this world. At the top are the *Tennin* (Heavenly Beings) who are divine but still have desires and are not beyond rebirth; then the *Ningen* (Humans); *Shura* (Warring Demons); *Chikusho* (Animals); *Gaki* (Hungry Spirits); and last *Jigoku* (Hell).

With the graveyards of the city now centered in the eastern hills, the red gate of Chinnoji is Kyoto's "Door to the Underworld." During *Obon*, thousands of people come to Chinnoji, bearing lotus flowers to offer to spirits of the dead. And while they're there, they take a peek at the well in the temple grounds through which it is said that Ono Takamura descended to the land of the dead. Deeper in the temple grounds but not usually shown to the public is another well—the one that Takamura used to come back up.

Part of the interest of temples such as Chinnoji, Marishiten, and Rokuharamitsuji is that they have a very "neighborhood" feel. The locals go there; the tourists don't. Kusaka's mounting studio stood in the middle of this neighborhood, and his son still lives there today. For him, Chinnoji is just the temple around the corner. Marishiten is in the block where he used to deliver newspapers

329

when he was a boy. For Kusaka and people like him living in old parts of town, temples like this—arcane relics that can hardly be found anywhere else in Japan—are intimate places, merged into their daily lives.

―――――――

Symbols Everywhere

What with *Ah Un*, Marishi's wild boars, Enma's black hat, the *rakan*'s dragon rising from his bowl, the "Six Ways," the multiple hands, heads, and eyes of the images at Sanjusangendo, and so forth, one is brought to think about symbolism. This is what French author Roland Barthes picked up on, except that he was only looking at Japan, and actually the importance of symbolism is pan-Asian. Naturally, we have important symbols in Western art but in East Asia symbols are everything. Whether it's Kabuki, Thai masked drama, or court dances from Java, every movement of the arms, hands, and legs means something. That's just not true for ballet or opera, in which it's the harmony of the whole that matters.

Oswald Spengler, in *The Decline of the West*, wrote that the string quartet was the supreme achievement of Western civilization because it's pure harmonics. The supreme achievement of the East would be, by contrast, a telling symbolic detail, such as the ritual hand gestures, *mudra*, of Hindu and Buddhist sculpture. In Java, these became the backward-bending fingers of court dancers, a concept passed on to Angkor in Cambodia, and Ayutthaya in Thailand, traveling all the way up to Japan, where a vestige still survives in the hand position of a Noh drama performer.

In each country, the *mudra* are telling us the same thing: that this dancer is not human, he or she is divine, an angel or a god from another world. This concept alone is enough to change one's feeling about the dance.

Symbolic meanings apply to rooflines, the layouts of buildings, costume, headwear, landscape painting, flower arranging—everything. In fact, a large proportion of this book is devoted to symbols and how to unravel and appreciate them. The symbols took time—centuries—to develop with their own internal logic; and it takes time to stop and gaze, and allow them to seep into our hearts and minds and do their deep and mysterious work. This brings us back to the *time* that it took to create these things, and the *time* it takes to appreciate them.

Even the seemingly simplest Zen garden is riven with symbols from other branches of Buddhism, such as Esoteric and Pure Land Buddhism.

For example, as a pure space removed from the mundane world, the enclosed plot is a microcosm of Heaven, that is, it's the Pure Land of the savior bodhisattva Amida (Pure Land).

In addition, we find elements from Chinese Confucianism and Daoism. The rocks depict *Horai-san* "The Isles of the Immortals," or the auspicious pair of the Tortoise and the Crane (Daoist). Meanwhile, in the pairing of rocks with sand, or piled-up earth and submerged pond, we see parallel concepts such as "Land and Sea," "Existence versus Void," and so forth (Confucianism).

There are also strong Shinto influences. The raked sand derives from the *saniwa*, "sand garden," where shamans would go into trance and call the spirits down to earth, as well as purificatory sand mounds in front of old shrines.

The extent to which these things can be seen in any one garden varies. Some places have no Tortoise or Crane; others have no sand or wall. On the other hand, there are gardens that include all of these symbolic elements at once. In any case, a supposedly "simple" and "abstract" Zen garden is anything but.

Although the symbols might be subliminal, they have the power to stir the soul in a way that a simple appeal to form and color, even the most sublime Spenglerian harmony, cannot.

Let's take another look at Sanjusangendo. The building and its contents make up one huge symbolic structure. Key to the design of Sanjusangendo is the concept of a *mandala*, a diagram, usually geometric, painted inside a square or circle, which illustrates a cosmic spiritual principle. Typically *mandala* take the form of paintings, with guardian figures painted at the outside edges, and gods of increasing importance arrayed in squares or circles inside. My Tibetan guru taught me that when you look at a *mandala*, you should approach it in stages. You travel into it, starting with the outside rings and working your way to the epiphany at the center.

In the case of Sanjusangendo, its creators built a three-dimensional *mandala*. A *mandala* of Compassion. Except that in this case, instead of designing the building in the round, they built it as one long horizontal progression. The better for pilgrims to experience it as a journey.

Just as in a *mandala* painting, a row of guardians poses dramatically at the front. Behind them, lined up on ten rising tiers, stand the one thousand images of Kannon, every figure with twenty arms at each side (plus two in front, clasped in prayer). The forty hands at the sides bear magical implements, such as "The Wheel of the Law," "The Flask of Tears," "The Whisk," "Indra's Trident," "The Sun," "The Moon," "The Rope to Bind Ignorance," etc. Every side arm represents twenty-five unseen arms, meaning that each image is symbolically wielding one thousand arms. With one thousand images, that's one million arms.

As you walk slowly down the corridor, you notice that these statues, while identical at first glance, all feature subtle differences. The way the hair is parted and arranged, the lines of falling drapery, the shape of faces and eyes, the line of the moustache, and the slight uplift of the smile, they're all different. After passing five hundred statues, you reach the center, where sits one grand Kannon, the one from whom it is all emanating. From here you once again pass by five hundred more images of Compassion, before finally emerging into the back corridor and then exiting the building.

If you take your time, and somehow ignore the ruckus from hordes of schoolchildren and tourists, the incremental power of symbolic imagery begins to sink in, to the point that in the end it's overwhelming. You can't help but marvel at the million ways that compassion makes itself felt in the world—and that's the point of the *mandala*.

Enma's Judgment Is Proclaimed

But let's return to Senbon Enma-do and its statue. On that day during *Obon*, I found myself standing in front of this enraged, colossal figure of the God of Hell glaring at me with those amber eyes snatched from the fires of the Onin War and roaring out of that gaping mouth.

As to whether he is a "must-see" sight of Kyoto, I wouldn't necessarily recommend him, and here's why. The statue was carved in 1488, and this makes it one of the older statues in the city. But it's crudely executed, a far cry from the sophistication and elegance that we usually associate with Kyoto. From that point of view, it's not an artistic highlight. It's the symbolism that's important and the medieval horrific power. This Enma hails from a time of plague, famine, war, fire, and earthquake. That's what this statue is.

It's not something to make a special detour to go and see. But if you are especially interested in old sculpture, or if you happen to be out along Senbon at the right time of year, and you feel Enma beckoning, then go, although it's not really a fun thing to do. Actually, it's mortifying. For Enma is not just about Death; he's about weighing and measuring Life.

I stood in front of the demonic triad. I felt naked, as if I'd met the old crone Datsueba on the way in, and she had stripped me of all excuses. King Enma spat out a peony, wordlessly, but I could hear him loud enough. I slunk away, and I may not be back to visit that statue for a while.

What was Enma's judgment, you ask? I'm not saying.

Where else could you have such a meeting with the "dreamtime" that you don't think about in your daily life as you run about answering the phone and writing e-mails? Suddenly you have these burning eyes bulging with a vision of death, and a furious, engorged, peony-spitting red mouth shouting at you: "What are you doing with your life?!"

You just can't get that except in a traditional place like Kyoto, because in modern towns, not only the obvious marks of contemporary life, like automobiles and apartment buildings, but even traditional art and religion have been homogenized, reduced to simplified basics. In America you'll find plenty of standard Churches of Christ, very few chapels dedicated to Saint Sebastian or the Madonna of the Grotto. Who would know what in the world these were? So even our religion, the last hold-out of non-rational ideas, is becoming generic. We no longer have time for dreamtime.

In Japan, the standard Buddhist halls of worship to Amida, Nichiren, and Zen abound and flourish, but nobody's building new temples to the Horse-Headed Kannon, or Marishiten, "God of Chance"; and if somebody did take the trouble to set up a new Sanjusangendo with a thousand Kannons, the figures would be extruded from plastic and all look exactly alike. These old things have no place in a rationally designed modern city. What civic planner would arrange—amongst the highways and subways, public parks, skyscrapers, convention halls, shopping centers, sports stadiums, and aquariums—for a little temple to the Lord of Hell?

Acknowledgements

Another Kyoto has taken time—time to reflect and time to enrich it with fresh insights. When we first conceived this project in 2004, we never expected it would take so long to complete. In 2007, we sent a sample chapter to Sekaibunkasha editor Sobhi Iida, who enthusiastically urged us on. Despite serial delays and constant rewriting, she never gave up. We are indebted to her for her patience, encouragement, and steadfast dedication.

For another pair of eyes to review the texts, Sobhi suggested *Kyoto Journal* editor Stuart Wachs who edited the version on which the book was eventually based. Kyoto author Robert Brady provided invaluable feedback.

Tokyo artist Tetsuji Fujihara created the drawings, and Vitsanu Riewseng provided additional illustrations. Kanazawa Yoshiko spent hundreds of hours looking up arcane facts in books and libraries to check our facts.

Lastly, we would like to thank our friends and families for trusting that all this time and effort would bear worthy fruit.